THE ARTHRITIS HANDBOOK

A Problem-Solving Approach to Arthritis Management

Library of Congress Catalog Card Number 74-9209

ISBN 911910-99-9

Printed in the United States of America

THE ARTHRITIS HANDBOOK

A Problem-Solving Approach to Arthritis Management

Joseph Lee Hollander, M.D.
Editor

Published by

Merck Sharp & Dohme
Division of Merck & Co., Inc.
West Point, Pa. 19486

1974

PUBLISHER'S NOTE

Merck Sharp & Dohme is privileged to participate in this major publishing effort with a distinguished group of authorities on rheumatology.

This publication combines innovative techniques in print communication with the medical expertise of the contributing authors. Our goal is to present a body of useful information on arthritic disorders in a practical format that offers easy access for the busy practitioner.

We also hope this publication will serve as a useful reference volume on selected drugs for the management of arthritic disorders. It is not intended that the drug information presented in the upcoming chapters should be the sole source of prescribing information for products mentioned. The current Direction Circulars must be regarded as the appropriate source of prescribing information, and the reader is urged to consult them before prescribing or administering any product.

Direction Circulars for Merck Sharp & Dohme products mentioned in this handbook may be found inserted in the inside back cover.

Merck Sharp & Dohme provided the resources for designing, printing, and distributing this handbook; however, the content represents the independent opinions and experiences of the authors and the editor, Dr. Joseph Lee Hollander. Individually and collectively, they deserve the full measure of credit for the value of this publishing effort.

FOREWORD

This book is written for the practitioner who knows little about rheumatology, but is faced with problems of musculoskeletal aches, pains, and swelling in his patients. It tries to answer the questions, "What is it?" and "What can I do to treat it?"

All textbooks of rheumatology, including the excellent *Primer on the Rheumatic Diseases*, available through the Arthritis Foundation, and our own large text, *Arthritis and Allied Conditions*, are diagnosis oriented. Determining the correct diagnosis from symptoms and signs may be as difficult as finding a friend's home without knowing the street and number. This book starts from the problems themselves, leading through the diagnostic processes and describing appropriate treatment. It is truly problem oriented, and goes along with the increasingly popular Weed System of problem-oriented patient evaluations.

The authors were chosen because of their wide and long expertise in their subjects. All have been attentive to the purpose of the book—to give practical material, literally to be a "do-it-yourself" guide to the field of arthritis and related disorders. The book cannot and does not attempt to cover all of the field of rheumatology. For example, discussions of experimental agents in treatment are omitted because they are not yet approved for regular use.

This volume emphasizes problems that are commonly seen in clinical practice. All of the authors practice and have faced the problems many times themselves. They have attempted to present the "tricks of the trade" to their colleagues. If the physician finds this book to be of practical everyday use in helping his patients with arthritis, we have succeeded in our endeavor.

Joseph Lee Hollander, M.D.
Editor

CONTRIBUTING AUTHORS

CHAPTER 1: Joseph Lee Hollander, M.D., M.A.C.P.

Professor of Medicine
School of Medicine
University of Pennsylvania
Philadelphia, Pennsylvania

CHAPTER 2: Currier McEwen, M.D., M.A.C.P.

Emeritus Professor of Medicine
New York University School of Medicine
New York, New York

Consulting Physician
Bellevue and University Hospitals, New York

Consulting Physician to
Regional Memorial Hospital, Brunswick, Maine;
Maine Medical Center, Portland, Maine;
Central Maine General Hospital, Lewiston, Maine;
and Veterans Administration Hospital, Togus, Maine

CHAPTER 3: Alan S. Cohen, M.D., F.A.C.P.

Conrad Wesselhoeft Professor of Medicine
Boston University School of Medicine
Boston, Massachusetts

Chief of Medicine and Director
Thorndike Memorial Laboratories
Boston City Hospital

Head, Section on Arthritis and
   Connective Tissue Diseases
Boston University Medical Center

CHAPTER 4: Richard H. Freyberg, M.D., M.A.C.P.

Emeritus Clinical Professor of Medicine and Chief
Division of Rheumatic Diseases
Cornell University Medical College
New York, New York

Emeritus Director
Department of Rheumatic Diseases
Hospital for Special Surgery
New York, New York

CHAPTER 5:   Robert L. Swezey, M.D., F.A.C.P.

Professor of Medicine and Rehabilitation Medicine
University of Southern California School of Medicine
Los Angeles, California

CHAPTER 6:   Norman O. Rothermich, M.D., F.A.C.P.

Clinical Professor of Medicine
The Ohio State University
Columbus, Ohio

Medical Director
Columbus Medical Center Research Foundation

CHAPTER 7:   Daniel J. McCarty, Jr., M.D., F.A.C.P.

Professor of Medicine and Head
Section of Arthritis and Metabolic Diseases
Department of Medicine
The University of Chicago
Pritzker School of Medicine
Chicago, Illinois

CHAPTER 8:   Lee Ramsay Straub, M.D., F.A.C.S.

Professor of Clinical Surgery
Cornell University Medical College
New York, New York

Attending Orthopaedic Surgeon
Hospital for Special Surgery
New York Hospital

Consultant
Bronx Veterans Administration Hospital

CHAPTER 9:   Charley J. Smyth, M.D., M.A.C.P.

Professor of Medicine and Head
Division of Rheumatic Diseases
University of Colorado School of Medicine
Denver, Colorado

TABLE OF CONTENTS

PROBLEM-ORIENTED INDEX

PROBLEM-ORIENTED INDEX

CHAPTER 1

Setting and Achieving
Practical Objectives
of Arthritis Management

Joseph Lee Hollander, M.D., M.A.C.P.
Professor of Medicine
School of Medicine
University of Pennsylvania
Philadelphia, Pennsylvania

CHAPTER 1

Setting and Achieving Practical Objectives of Arthritis Management

Joseph Lee Hollander, M.D., M.A.C.P.

A. Introduction

To treat any form of arthritis effectively, the diagnosis must be established first. This, of course, is obvious to any intelligent physician. Just as it is impossible to find a telephone number without knowing the spelling of the name, so it is impossible to devise proper treatment without knowing the type of arthritis. But how can a specific diagnosis be achieved? To help answer that question, this book "starts from scratch" with the symptoms, signs, and problems the physician detects in his patients. It then considers how to diagnose clinically from those problems, and reviews laboratory tests and x-ray diagnostic aids that can help to confirm the clinical impression.

When an accurate diagnosis is made early in the disease process, treatment can begin promptly, starting with general and conservative measures. In terms of treatment, this book discusses physical management and appropriate drugs for each of many arthritic problems, along with possible complications that may accompany each mode of therapy. Special measures, such as intra-articular steroid therapy, are described, with a discussion of when, how, and why to use them and the possible adverse effects and dangers to watch for. How to manage complications or special situations and when to call in an orthopedic surgeon are considered next. Finally, how the physician can evaluate the success or failure of therapy is considered, with a

3

discussion of alternate courses of treatment to consider when therapy is not producing the desired results.

The key to usefulness of this book is the Problem-Oriented Index. Here the usual presenting symptoms are listed with the page numbers where each symptom is discussed, both diagnostically and therapeutically.

Essentially this book is "do-it-yourself rheumatology." It is not another textbook on arthritis and other rheumatic diseases. The combined effort of the authors is to make it easier for the physician to proceed confidently and effectively in coping with arthritic problems, so that the patient receives the best possible treatment, initially and continually, with minimum delay, cost, and risk of harmful effects.

Many forms of arthritis are chronic and incurable, and the cause often is unknown. But this does not mean that we should throw up our hands in despair and neglect the arthritic patient. There are many effective measures that not only relieve suffering from these painful afflictions, but also arrest progression and prevent destruction of joints, crippling, and loss of function. Even where there has been damage to joints or other structures responsible for motion, there are many effective measures for rehabilitation which can restore function. Amazingly helpful corrective operations for damaged joints have been developed and perfected over the past decade.

Naturally, the primary physician is not expected to carry out complicated programs or operations himself, but the promptly applicable forms of therapy are laid out simply in this volume. Equally important to the physician is recognition of special problems and complications that require hospitalization or help from a specialist. The reasons for the existence of specialists are the in-depth knowledge, experience, and judgment they acquire for dealing with complicated situations, and the special skills and techniques they can use to cope with them. Many arthritic patients can be treated effectively throughout protracted disease. But the physician must know when to do what—whether it be diagnosis, treatment, or referral.

B. Defining Arthritic Problems

Painful disorders of the musculoskeletal system are all forms of rheumatism, but arthritis is the term used when the joints are the primary site of pain, swelling, stiffness, or limitation of motion. The patient knows where it hurts, but the physician has to determine from the history and examination exactly which parts are involved. For example, a pain in the shoulder could mean arthritis of the shoulder joint, bursitis of the subdeltoid bursa, tendinitis of the supraspinatus or long bicipital tendons, myositis of the trapezius, rhomboid, or levator scapulae muscles, or even referred pain from arthritis of the neck. The localization of pain, tenderness, or limited motion can help make the anatomical diagnosis, even though the problem may be part of a more widespread disease process.

When taking the history, the physician may find it helpful to ask the following questions:

- When did you first notice the pain (swelling, stiffness, etc.)?
- Did it start suddenly, or did you gradually become aware of it?
- Had you been ill in any other way when it started?
- Had you been doing anything unusual before it began? (Unaccustomed activities leading to strain or trauma often are forgotten.)
- When does it bother you most? (Pain may be noted only on certain movements, only at night, only on arising in the morning, after sitting for long periods, later in the day, with fatigue, or constantly.)
- Describe the pain; is it sharp, aching, dull, a soreness?
- Is the pain just in one spot or does it seem to spread down the arm (or back or leg)? (Pain often is referred along nerve trunks, muscles or tendons distally: e.g. hip pain may refer to the knee, lower leg; back pain into the extremities, etc.)
- Do your symptoms wake you from sleep or keep you from going to sleep?
- Have you felt weak or tired; have you lost your appetite?
- Is the pain getting worse, staying the same, or is it less severe than when it started?
- Has the pain spread to other joints or areas of your body?
- What have you found that helps relieve it? (Rest, heat, aspirin, liniment, etc.)

The physical signs of joint disease may appear complex, but they are easy to learn. Excellent detailed descriptions can be found in our textbook[1] or in a monograph by Beetham et al.,[2] so only the rudiments are given here. Each symptomatic joint or group of joints should be examined for the following:

- *Skin abnormalities* about the area (e.g., heat, redness, sweating, skin eruptions, ulcers).
- *Swelling:* periarticular edema near the joint, synovial thickening (a doughy enlargement limited to the joint area), joint effusion (a fluctuant or tense swelling), or bony enlargement.
- *Tenderness* on palpation, diffuse or localized, slight or marked.
- *Crepitation:* palpable rubbing sensation, grating or crackling on motion.
- *Limitation of motion:* movement, both active and passive, as compared with contralateral side or with normal range.

- □ *Deformity* from contractures, subluxation, bony absorption, or bony enlargement.
- □ *Changes in muscles about the joint:* weakness, spasm, contractures, or atrophy.
- □ *Nodules or localized swelling near the joint:* e.g., rheumatoid nodules near elbows; gouty tophi on fingers, toes, elbows, etc.; ganglia near wrist; or even palpable loose bodies in the knee.

The arthritic problem may be anywhere and everywhere, ranging from a painful jaw to a sore toe, from generalized aching and stiffness to a swollen finger. The distribution of joint involvement is extremely important where multiple joints are affected. Bilateral involvement of the same joints (symmetrical joint involvement) is significant, suggesting rheumatoid arthritis. Certain joints may suggest certain diagnoses. For example, knee involvement in an obese patient who is middle-aged or older suggests osteoarthritis.

Other factors to consider are the patient's occupation, which may cause strains on some joints, and whether the onset of symptoms is acute or insidious and the joint involvement progressive—migratory in rheumatic fever, spreading centrifugally from the spine to extremities in ankylosing spondylitis, or centripetally from small joints of extremities toward larger joints in rheumatoid arthritis. Acute recurrent attacks (episodic arthritis) seen in gout or palindromic rheumatism are vastly different from the slow and fairly steady progression to more joints in rheumatoid arthritis.

After taking the history and examining his patient, the physician may still be in a quandary about diagnosis. Chapters 2 and 3 are designed to help in this situation. When in doubt, consult the Problem-Oriented Index. It should be noted that x-rays are seldom helpful in diagnosing any type of arthritis in the early stages.

C. Dealing with the Arthritic Patient

Any arthritic patient seeking help from his physician is afraid. He is frightened by the pain and stiffness which often interfere with sleep, make him feel weak and miserable, and, most of all, threaten his ability to continue his normal way of life. In every patient, young or old, male or female, this fear is the factor that leads him to the physician, often after long hesitation and reluctance. "What is happening to me?" and "What will happen to me?" are his fundamental worries, whether the condition is a sore foot, painful shoulder, backache, or generalized aching and stiffness. In some this fear reaches the proportions of panic.

As soon as the doctor reaches at least a working diagnosis, his first task is to reassure his patient. This cannot be a perfunctory "brush-off" of the problem or an offhand assurance of a "cure." In most instances such statements will make the patient distrust the physician, even though it is welcome news. Such appraisals put the physician under an obligation to make good his promise or lose the confidence of the patient. Even when the physician knows the condition is self-limited, it is unwise to be over-optimistic because unforeseen complications may develop.

On the other hand, it is cruel to be too pessimistic by warning the patient of all the horrible things that might develop. Some physicians prefer to be pessimistic: "Expect the worst and you'll never be disappointed." They feel that whatever happens they will look better by being pessimistic—if the patient does poorly, he has been warned beforehand; if he does well, the physician has pulled him out of a horrible mess and deserves great credit. This attitude can be devastating to the patient. He may go into panic, adding neurosis to his organic disease. In Chapter 4, on the general measures used in the management of arthritis, Dr. Freyberg discusses the need for "guarded optimism"—maintaining the confidence of the patient and continuing to encourage him as a part of treatment.

D. Objectives of Arthritis Treatment

Goals for management must be realistic. Many forms of arthritis are chronic and incurable. The physician will do well to recall the traditional aim of treatment: "To cure a few, to help many, and to comfort all." I clearly remember the gratitude of one hopelessly crippled rheumatoid arthritic patient for the little help I could give her. She had been confined to a bed and wheelchair for a dozen years by ankylosed hips, knees, ankles, wrists, left shoulder and elbow, and many finger joints—a fate all too many rheumatoid patients suffered in the years B.C. (before cortisone). She was a talented artist in spite of her handicaps, having been able to paint with her slightly movable right shoulder and elbow and holding the brush with difficulty in her gnarled fingers.

When she was admitted to the hospital in 1951, she was very depressed. Her right shoulder and elbow had become acutely swollen and painful, preventing her from painting. This was the year intra-articular corticosteroid therapy was introduced. Injections into her right shoulder and elbow suppressed the inflammation, allowing her to regain function with the help of physical therapy in both joints. Pain was diminished. She could once more feed herself and, more important to her, she could resume painting. Five of her beautiful paintings hang in my home and office, presented in gratitude for restoring her limited function.

No matter to her that she couldn't walk; she could paint again. No matter to her that the injections had to be repeated every few weeks for the next seven years to prevent recurrence of the dreadful pain and swelling; she was happy and productive until her death from a myocardial infarction at age 62.

This anecdote illustrates the four major objectives of therapy:
- Sustained relief of pain and stiffness in joints and muscles.
- Reduction or suppression of inflammation.
- Preservation of function of affected parts.
- Prevention of contractures or ankylosis.

Patients with chronic arthritis do not expect miracles, but they do expect relief of pain and they need continued help and encouragement. The goals of therapy must be realistic. Aiming too high will result in disappointment and depression. On the other hand, the physician who tells his patient, "I am sorry, but there is nothing I can do for you," is cruel and thoughtless. There is almost always something that can be done to help every arthritic patient, particularly in this day of orthopedic corrective operations and rehabilitation (see Chapters 5 and 8). Furthermore, chronic arthritis is not always relentless and lifelong, so the prognosis must not be made too pessimistic. The variable and often unpredictable course of rheumatoid arthritis makes it virtually impossible to give an accurate prognosis except for short terms.

Sustained relief of pain can be obtained in many ways, depending on the type of arthritis. Means of obtaining relief of pain are discussed in detail in Chapters 4, 5, 6, and 7. Specific cases may be found through the Problem-Oriented Index. Mere relief of pain is not the only objective, however, as even opiates and acupuncture can blot out pain but do not have any effect on the irritation or inflammatory reaction that causes it.

Reduction or suppression of inflammation is a necessary part of any arthritis therapeutic program. This may be accomplished by rest of the inflamed part, by physical therapy, or by use of anti-inflammatory agents. Continued inflammation—whether the low-grade response to friction as in osteoarthritis or the more exudative and severe inflammatory response seen in rheumatoid arthritis, gout, or septic arthritis—gradually or rapidly produces deterioration of cartilage and surrounding joint structures. This leads to destruction of the joint with loss of function, contractures, or even ankylosis. The products of the inflammatory reaction accumulate in the joint, tending to prolong the reaction, which can change the condition from acute to chronic. Suppressing the inflammation early in its course may nip this problem in the bud.

Too many physicians have become therapeutic nihilists from experiences they have had with side effects from the more potent anti-inflammatory agents, particularly corticosteroids. After 25 years of clinical use, it has become clear that the steroids are the most potent agents available for control of *severe* arthritic inflammation. Such drugs have been much abused, and no one should minimize their potential dangers; but they often prevent ankylosis of joints and preserve function, side effects notwithstanding.

Corticosteroid therapy does not prevent progression of the erosive lesions of rheumatoid arthritis and often introduces new and serious complications, such as osteoporosis (see Chapter 6). Unstable joints are amenable to orthopedic correction and, even with deformities, joint function often can be preserved or restored (see Chapter 8).

If the involved joint or joints can be moved, albeit with limitations from pain or weakness, the muscles controlling the joint are less likely to develop contractures or atrophy and joint function can be preserved. Only the very acutely involved joints require splinting or complete bed rest. Careful and relatively painless exercises can be instituted early (see Chapter 5).

Abuse of inflamed joints can lead to such deformities as subluxations and instability. Too complete or prolonged immobilization, on the other hand, can lead to contractures or even ankylosis with loss of joint function. The proper balance between rest and exercise is difficult to achieve in some patients, but must be frequently evaluated and prescribed for all.

E. Summary

It is necessary to obtain pain relief to preserve function, and it is necessary to continue function to prevent deformity. Measures to relieve pain and suppress inflammation can be, and often are, abused. Measures to preserve function are often neglected, but sometimes are abused also. Measures to prevent deformity are often neglected and rarely abused, but are all too frequently unsuccessful in severe and unremitting chronic arthritis. These three objectives are interdependent. Each is vital, but the most important long-term goal of treatment is preservation of function. The physician who has treated his patient for many years for a severe, chronic, incurable arthritis can realize great satisfaction from seeing his patient still able to carry out his daily activities, minor deformities and continued mild pain notwithstanding.

REFERENCES

1. Lockie, L. M.: Examination of the arthritic patient. In Arthritis and Allied Conditions, *ed. J. L. Hollander and D. J. McCarty, Jr., 8th edition, Philadelphia, Lea & Febiger, 1972, pp. 15-25.*

2. Beetham, W. P., Polley, H. F., Slocumb, C. H., and Weaver, W. F.: Physical Examination of Joints, *Philadelphia, W. B. Saunders Company, 1965.*

CHAPTER 2

A Logical Approach
to the Differential
Diagnosis of Arthritis

Currier McEwen, M.D., M.A.C.P.
Emeritus Professor of Medicine
New York University School of Medicine
New York, New York

Consulting Physician, Bellevue and University Hospitals, New York

Consulting Physician to Regional Memorial Hospital, Brunswick, Maine;
Maine Medical Center, Portland, Maine; Central Maine General Hospital, Lewiston,
Maine; and Veterans Administration Hospital, Togus, Maine

CHAPTER 2

A Logical Approach to the Differential Diagnosis of Arthritis

Currier McEwen, M.D., M.A.C.P.

In arthritis, as in most diseases, the difficulty of diagnosis can vary from those cases in which it is at once self-evident to those in which even careful observation over long periods may still leave doubt. This, of course, depends on the characteristic features of the various types of arthritis which may be present. In this chapter, differential diagnosis of arthritis and disorders causing similar complaints will be presented in the framework of the types of problems which are encountered in daily practice. The following problems will be considered:

A. Arthritis of Acute Onset

Most cases of this type fall into one of the following categories:
- rheumatic fever
- acute gouty arthritis
- pyogenic arthritis
- rheumatoid arthritis
- Reiter's disease
- systemic lupus erythematosus
- psoriatic arthritis
- arthritis associated with periodic illnesses
- foreign protein reactions
- pseudogout
- arthritis associated with ulcerative colitis and regional enteritis
- viral arthritis
- ankylosing spondylitis
- erythema nodosum
- anaphylactoid purpura
- leukemia
- sickle cell disease
- hemophilia
- acute periarthritis and shoulder-hand syndrome

This is a formidable list, but in most instances differentiation can be made relatively quickly.

1. Rheumatic fever

When other features of rheumatic fever, such as carditis, erythema marginatum, or characteristic rheumatic subcutaneous nodules, are present in a young person, the diagnosis can be made with great assurance. In the absence of these features, fever, coupled with migratory polyarthritis, is very suggestive. The arthritic symptoms typically include acutely painful swelling, overlying erythema, and gradual subsidence of arthritis in joints first affected as new ones become involved. It must be emphasized that evidence of carditis is very often lacking. Electrocardiographic signs of pericarditis or a prolonged PR interval may be present, but their absence is of no diagnostic significance. A rising antistreptolysin O titer indicates a recent hemolytic streptococcal infection, and does not necessarily mean rheumatic fever. Conversely, a persistently normal titer of antistreptolysin, especially if tests for other streptococcal antibodies also remain normal, is strong evidence against the diagnosis of rheumatic fever. Rapid erythrocyte sedimentation rates and increased titers of C-reactive protein, of course, merely indicate inflammation and are not otherwise diagnostic. A dramatic disappearance of pain, swelling, and erythema following full doses of aspirin also points to rheumatic fever, although some cases of acute rheumatoid arthritis can also show a similar initial response.

2. Acute gouty arthritis

The definitive diagnostic feature of acute gouty arthritis is the characteristic urate crystals in the synovial fluid. Highly suggestive is the typical red, indurated, extremely painful swelling of only one or two joints and a dramatic response to colchicine. A high serum urate level provides supporting evidence, but is not conclusive per se, especially if only moderately elevated, because some nongouty individuals have hyperuricemia. Moreover, most patients with painful joints have taken aspirin before they consult a physician. Since small doses of aspirin can cause hyperuricemia, many patients without gout have increased serum urate levels when first seen.

3. Pyogenic arthritis

By the time the patient sees a physician, acute arthritis due to invasion of the joint by a pyogenic microorganism usually has settled in one or two larger joints, which are acutely painful, swollen, and erythematous. Careful questioning, however, usually will reveal a history of rather mild, transient involvement of several other joints a few days earlier. This is especially true in gonococcal arthritis. Fever and other evidences of systemic infection and inflammation usually are present. Although aspirin in full doses may cause a marked fall in fever, it will have little effect on the arthritis. The definitive diagnostic feature is, of course, the demonstration of the causative microorganism in the joint fluid, either in direct smear or by culture.

4. Rheumatoid arthritis

Although rheumatoid arthritis most commonly begins insidiously or subacutely, acute onsets are by no means rare. Indeed, such onsets may lead to an early diagnosis of rheumatic fever. X-ray study and laboratory tests give little diagnostic help at this stage. Usually the diagnosis must be tentative for a week or two, when the evolving course of the disease makes its true nature apparent.

5. Reiter's disease

The arthritis of Reiter's disease is commonly rather acute in onset. Since there are no specific tests for it, diagnosis depends on the clinical features and course. When several other manifestations, such as urethritis, ocular inflammation, circinate balanitis, other mucous membrane lesions, or keratodermia blenorrhagicum, are present, diagnosis is relatively simple. However, few rheumatologists today would insist on the presence of the complete triad—urethritis, conjunctivitis, and arthritis—which formerly was demanded for diagnosis. A special problem is presented by the patient whose urethral discharge contains gonococci. Simultaneous occurrence of Reiter's disease and gonococcal infection is not rare. If the urethritis responds to penicillin but the arthritis does not, Reiter's disease is probable, and the presence of conjunctivitis, balanitis, or keratodermia makes that diagnosis secure.

6. Systemic lupus erythematosus

Acute onsets of arthritis are not the rule in systemic lupus erythematosus, but they may occur. Fever, rash, and other features of the disease, and a positive antinuclear antibody test with peripheral pattern confirm the diagnosis.

7. Psoriatic arthritis

This form of joint disease often starts rather acutely. The most important diagnostic feature is, of course, concurrent psoriatic changes in skin or nails. Occasionally the arthritis appears first and, in such instances, the correct diagnosis usually becomes clear only after the evolution of typical cutaneous lesions. However, psoriatic arthritis can be suspected earlier if the arthritis is asymmetrical, and especially if the distal interphalangeal joints are involved.

8. Arthritis associated with periodic illnesses

So-called palindromic rheumatism, intermittent hydrarthrosis, and arthritis accompanying familial Mediterranean fever all may start acutely. In all of these conditions, the diagnosis is first suggested by the periodic nature of the attacks. The particular label to attach depends on the special features of the individual illnesses.[1]

9. Foreign protein reactions

Arthritis of this type formerly resulted from injections of antisera, but today are more commonly the result of penicillin administration. When the arthritis is accompanied by urticaria, the diagnosis is evident. In those cases without urticaria or when arthritis occurs first, diagnosis may be extremely difficult. A special and not uncommon problem is presented by arthritis occurring in patients who have received an inadequate course of penicillin, given for less than ten days, for hemolytic streptococcal throat infection. Whether such arthritis is due to rheumatic fever or to a penicillin reaction may remain uncertain unless some distinctive feature of rheumatic fever appears or urticaria develops.

10. Pseudogout

Attacks simulating gout in middle-aged or elderly patients with normal serum urate levels make one think of pseudogout. Such attacks usually do not respond to colchicine. As in gout, the definitive diagnostic test is examination of the synovial fluid, which in pseudogout reveals the presence of calcium pyrophosphate crystals.[2]

11. Arthritis associated with ulcerative colitis and regional enteritis
The peripheral arthritis associated with these intestinal diseases very often is acute in onset and may suggest rheumatic fever. When colitic features are present, the diagnosis is fairly apparent. However, in some 10 percent of cases, the first attack of arthritis occurs before the onset of recognizable ulcerative colitis.[3] In such cases diagnosis is aided by the fact that, in ulcerative colitis, the arthritis is less migratory than in rheumatic fever and usually only two or three joints are involved in a single attack. The failure of the antistreptolysin titer to rise in serial tests also is helpful, but the true nature may remain uncertain in some cases until the intestinal disease becomes apparent.

12. Viral arthritis
Arthritis occurring in rubella, in other viral diseases, or after immunization against rubella often starts abruptly, although the inflammation usually is not very severe. At onset, viral arthritis cannot be differentiated clinically from rheumatoid arthritis, but the transient course and its relationship to viral infection or immunization point to the correct diagnosis.[4]

13. Ankylosing spondylitis
This is rarely a cause of acute symptoms in peripheral joints. Occasionally, however, sudden, severe pain in a knee or other large joint may occur before symptoms appear that are referable to the back. (See also section G-5, page 29.)

14. Erythema nodosum
Arthritis, sometimes acute in onset, occurs in 60 to 75 percent of patients with erythema nodosum. The arthritic symptoms often precede the characteristic cutaneous lesions and thus make initial diagnosis difficult.[5] These lesions are tender, indurated, and erythematous and usually appear on the shins; with their appearance the diagnosis is clear. However, the presence of erythema nodosum demands careful search for other diseases, notably ulcerative colitis, regional enteritis, and sarcoidosis, which are characterized by erythema nodosum and arthritis.

15. Anaphylactoid purpura
16. Leukemia
17. Sickle cell disease
18. Hemophilia

Arthritic manifestations of these diseases are more commonly seen in children than in adults and are discussed in section K of this chapter.

19. Acute periarthritis and shoulder-hand syndrome
These common disorders are discussed in section H.

B. Monarticular Arthritis

Any form of arthritis may be monarticular at onset. Indeed, a single joint may be involved in rheumatoid arthritis and psoriatic arthritis for six months or even longer. Bearing this in mind, one may say that persistent monarticular arthritis usually is due to the following:

- gout
- pseudogout
- pyogenic arthritis
- mechanical injury
- tuberculous arthritis
- osteoarthritis
- avascular necrosis
- osteoid osteoma
- malignant tumors

1. Gout
2. Pseudogout
3. Pyogenic arthritis

These disorders are often monarticular, but usually are distinguished from other monarticular arthritides by their acuteness. The definitive diagnostic features are noted in the preceding discussion of acute arthritis.

4. Mechanical injury

These cases vary from acute and subacute episodes closely following obvious injury to milder attacks occurring some time after injury. Sometimes the injury is so minor that it goes unnoticed. In the absence of a known, direct trauma, diagnosis may be made only by exclusion, and will require that the course of the disease be followed for weeks or months. Bloody or xanthrochromic synovial fluid aids diagnosis in the early stages. X-ray study usually reveals effusion. Laboratory examination of the joint fluid usually shows a low white count and normal viscosity. The erythrocyte sedimentation rate is lower than would be expected in arthritis that is primarily inflammatory. In recurrent and persistent cases, when the probable correctness of diagnosis warrants exploratory surgery, the nature of the disability usually becomes apparent.

5. Tuberculous arthritis

Although tuberculous arthritis is no longer very common, it must be borne seriously in mind, especially in subacute and chronic monarticular cases. Diagnosis is especially important in this condition because treatment by intra-articular injection of corticosteroids can be disastrous. Tubercle bacilli can very rarely be identified by direct smear of synovial fluid, but the culture can be diagnostic even though its growth may not be positive for several weeks. Positive needle biopsy is diagnostic, but negative results mean little. When in doubt, open biopsy for careful histologic study is in order.

6. Osteoarthritis

Osteoarthritis secondary to old mechanical or inflammatory injury is a common cause of chronic monarticular arthritis. Swelling of bony type, x-ray evidence of cartilage thinning, and bony spurring are characteristic. The erythrocyte sedimentation rate may be normal or moderately rapid, depending on the absence or presence of secondarily induced synovitis. In most cases, synovial effusion is not apparent clinically, but may occur as a result of secondary synovitis. If present, its character may vary considerably, depending on the degree of synovial inflammation. Involvement of the hip is common, but the pain is frequently referred to the knee. Indeed, pain in a knee which physical examination shows to be normal is most often due to osteoarthritis of the corresponding hip.

7. Avascular necrosis

This may result from such obvious causes as caisson disease, prolonged administration of large doses of corticosteroids, a fracture of the neck of the femur, and sickle cell disease. It may also occur without any apparent explanation. The head of the femur is the most common site, where the disease gives rise to a slowly increasing pain in the hip, often with radiation to the knee, and progressive limitation of motion. Diagnosis is made by the characteristic changes seen on x-ray.

8. Osteoid osteoma

This uncommon disease has predeliction for the long bones and may be mistaken for arthritis when the lesion is near a joint. Characteristic features are the slowly increasing pain, which in time may become extremely severe, the lack of any swelling or local heat, and normal laboratory tests. The diagnosis is suggested by finding a circumscribed radiolucent lesion, rarely more than two centimeters in diameter, and is confirmed by biopsy.

9. Malignant tumors

Malignant tumors arising within a joint or from a bone adjacent to a joint may be mistaken for arthritis. Definitive diagnosis, of course, is made by biopsy.

C. Subacute or Chronic Arthritis of Multiple Joints, without Deformity Other than Swelling

Patients with arthritis of this type present very common diagnostic problems. Most cases fall into the following categories:
- rheumatoid arthritis
- systemic lupus erythematosus

- □ subacute gouty arthritis
- □ psoriatic arthritis
- □ arthritis associated with ulcerative colitis and regional enteritis
- □ Reiter's disease
- □ ankylosing spondylitis
- □ osteoarthritis
- □ viral arthritis
- □ hypertrophic osteoarthropathy
- □ sarcoidosis

1. Rheumatoid arthritis

This disorder is overwhelmingly the most common cause of subacute or chronic arthritis. Symmetrical involvement is characteristic, but the condition may begin asymmetrically. Periarticular soft-tissue swelling often is present, but swelling is chiefly intra-articular with effusion. Involvement of proximal interphalangeal and metacarpophalangeal joints is particularly suggestive. Roentgenologic examination may reveal soft-tissue swelling and juxta-articular osteoporosis only or, in more advanced disease, some cartilagenous thinning and bony erosions may be seen. Laboratory studies reveal moderate to marked increases in sedimentation rate. A test for rheumatoid factors frequently is positive, but a negative test in no way precludes the diagnosis. If characteristic subcutaneous nodules are present on the extensor surface of the forearm just distal to the olecranon processes, the diagnosis is essentially certain.

2. Systemic lupus erythematosus

Arthralgia and arthritis with swelling are among the common early manifestations of systemic lupus erythematosus. The arthritis may closely resemble that of rheumatoid disease, but fever and other systemic manifestations usually are decidedly more pronounced. When other features of lupus, such as butterfly or disseminated erythematous rash or nephritis, are present, the diagnosis is obvious. A positive lupus erythematosus test or antinuclear antibody test with peripheral type of pattern confirms the diagnosis.

3. Subacute gouty arthritis

Acute gouty arthritis involving only one or two joints can seldom cause a diagnostic problem, but occasional subacute cases involving multiple joints can simulate arthritis of other types. In such cases, a history of typical acute episodes recovering without residual damage, coupled with elevated serum uric acid, point to the correct diagnosis. The diagnosis is confirmed by finding urate crystals in the synovial fluid.

4. Psoriatic arthritis

This condition often mimics rheumatoid arthritis. In the great majority of cases, the characteristic lesions on the skin and nails make the diagnosis clear. In rare cases in which arthritis precedes the other features, involvement of distal interphalangeal joints gives strong supporting evidence if Heberden's nodes can be excluded. Psoriatic arthritis usually is asymmetrical.

5. Arthritis associated with ulcerative colitis and regional enteritis
The subacute examples of this disease are differentiated from other arthritides by the same features that distinguish the acute attacks discussed in section A-11.

6. Reiter's disease
This too is distinguished in its subacute form by the same features which help in diagnosis of acute attacks (see section A-5, page 17). Also suggestive of Reiter's disease are swelling and tenderness of the Achilles tendon at its point of insertion into the os calcis, and persistent pain in heels and feet on weight bearing after other obvious articular symptoms have subsided.

7. Ankylosing spondylitis
See section G-5.

8. Osteoarthritis
Although osteoarthritis secondary to an old injury or other articular abnormality characteristically affects only one or two joints (section B-6), primary osteoarthritis involves multiple joints, notably the distal interphalangeals of the fingers (causing Heberden's nodes) and the carpometacarpal joints of the thumbs. The knees frequently are involved and about 20 percent of patients with Heberden's nodes also have involvement of the proximal interphalangeals, which suggests rheumatoid arthritis. Swelling of knees and proximal interphalangeal joints is not infrequently fluctuant due to synovial effusion. Such cases especially must be distinguished from rheumatoid arthritis. X-ray examination usually shows the predominantly bony enlargement. Although older patients with rheumatoid arthritis of proximal interphalangeal joints may also have coincidental Heberden's nodes, the occurrence of proximal interphalangeal swelling and Heberden's nodes warrants the suspicion that both are due to osteoarthritis.

9. Viral arthritis
This fairly common arthritis associated with rubella infection and immunization (section A-12) is more often subacute than acute. The rarer examples of arthritis associated with lymphogranuloma venereum are more persistent, but are also nondestructive. This type is distinguished by the presence of venereal disease.

10. Hypertrophic osteoarthropathy

This most commonly causes aching in the regions of the long bones between the joints, but arthralgias also occur. Obvious swelling and pain of several joints frequently occur, which may suggest rheumatoid arthritis. The correct diagnosis is at once suggested by the periosteal changes of hypertrophic osteoarthropathy in roentgenograms. Chest films will often reveal a pulmonary neoplasm. Clubbing of fingers may or may not be present.

11. Sarcoidosis

This rare form of arthritis is diagnosed by the presence of other manifestations, such as cutaneous and pulmonary lesions, by a positive Kveim test and by biopsy.[6]

D. Chronic Arthritis of Multiple Joints with Obvious Deformities

The principal arthritides of this type are as follows:
- rheumatoid arthritis
- psoriatic arthritis
- osteoarthritis
- systemic lupus erythematosus
- Reiter's disease
- arthritis associated with ulcerative colitis and regional enteritis
- chronic gouty arthritis
- ankylosing spondylitis
- sarcoidosis
- neurogenic arthropathy

1. Rheumatoid arthritis

This disease is the most common form of chronic arthritis. All of the features noted in section C-1 are applicable to diagnosis in these patients. Tests for rheumatoid factor are positive in some 85 percent of cases.[7] X-ray evidence of subluxation and cartilagenous and bony erosions is usually helpful. Ulnar deviation deformity at the metacarpophalangeal joints is particularly characteristic.

2. Psoriatic arthritis

In most cases psoriatic joint involvement ultimately results in deforming arthritis. Rarely, however, does it cause diagnostic difficulty because by the time deformities are present the cutaneous disease makes the nature of the arthritis clear.

3. Osteoarthritis

The primary type of osteoarthritis described in section C-8 often progresses to a stage in which proximal interphalangeal damage causes severe destruction of cartilage and creates bony erosions that mimic rheumatoid arthritis. Indeed, erosive osteoarthritis may ultimately result in bony anky- losis.[8] Such cases are commonly mistaken for rheumatoid arthritis. If the fact that osteoarthritis may cause this type of deformity is borne in mind, the features characterizing the two diseases will usually make the distinc- tion clearly apparent.

4. Systemic lupus erythematosus
The arthritis of systemic lupus may rarely progress to a stage of gross deformity clinically indistinguishable from rheumatoid arthritis. The fact that tests for rheumatoid factors frequently are positive in systemic lupus, and the lupus erythematosus test and antinuclear antibody test may be positive in rheumatoid arthritis, adds to the difficulty in diagnosis. Usually only the presence of other features of lupus makes the diagnosis certain.

5. Reiter's disease
In the great majority of cases, the arthritis of Reiter's disease subsides after several months without significant permanent damage. Rarely, however, it may become chronically deforming. The distinguishing diagnostic feature is the previous course accompanied by other features of Reiter's disease.

6. Arthritis associated with ulcerative colitis and regional enteritis
In rare instances these diseases can progress to stages of deformity. The diagnosis is made by the presence of the intestinal disease.

7. Chronic gouty arthritis
In its advanced stages, the arthritis of gout may simulate the deformities of rheumatoid arthritis to a striking extent. Tophi at the elbow may even sug- gest rheumatoid nodules. The correct diagnosis should always be apparent, however, from the history of repeated attacks recovering without residual damage and by the demonstration of urate crystals in tophi and synovial fluid.

8. Ankylosing spondylitis
This disorder can lead to deformity, most notably of hips and shoulders. However, by the time these symptoms appear, the spinal changes are obvious and the diagnosis is rarely in doubt.

9. Sarcoidosis
In rare instances the arthritis of sarcoidosis progresses to gross deformity. Diagnosis rests on biopsy and a positive Kveim test.

10. Neurogenic arthropathy
The so-called Charcot's joint was formerly seen chiefly as a result of tabes dorsalis. Today, with a declining number of tabes patients, the condition is

more often caused by syringomyelia and diabetic neuropathy. It is distinguished by its relatively painless course, the presence of the causative neurologic disorder, and particularly by the x-ray picture of articular disintegration.

E. Nonarticular Rheumatic Symptoms

This large group of patients includes many with fairly straightforward disabilities ranging from radiculitis due to low back strain, degenerative disc disease, and herniated discs, to mild, transient disorders such as muscular aching following unfamiliar exercise and the similar aching and arthralgias associated with infectious diseases. Other examples of nonarticular rheumatism that are less well understood will be considered briefly under the following headings:
  □ fibrositis
  □ psychogenic rheumatism
  □ polymyalgia rheumatica
  □ polymyositis and dermatomyositis
  □ periarthritis of the shoulder and shoulder-hand syndrome
  □ neuropathies

1. Fibrositis

Most rheumatologists will agree that this term is extremely vague and may mean different things to different physicians. It is sometimes carelessly designated as the reason for pain from other causes, such as radiculitis. In any case, the term is a misnomer, since there is no evidence to support the view that inflammatory changes are present in the fibrous connective tissue of patients in whom the diagnosis of fibrositis is made. In spite of these shortcomings, fibrositis has become established as a term applicable to vague aching and pain in areas around and between joints for which no other cause can be found, and in the presence of a normal or very slightly elevated erythrocyte sedimentation rate. Occasionally, inflammatory types of rheumatic disease, such as rheumatoid arthritis and systemic lupus, may start with vague aching. This may suggest fibrositis, but the increased sedimentation rate and other features of those diseases soon make the diagnosis clear. (See also psychogenic rheumatism below.)

2. Psychogenic rheumatism

This term is no less difficult to define than fibrositis; indeed, some rheumatologists use the terms synonymously. The diagnosis is used for nonarticular pain and arthralgia in patients with conversion psychological reactions and for vague connective tissue pain, possibly due to chronically increased muscle tension, in patients experiencing anxiety and emotional tension. Patients with fibrositis are worse after inactivity, improve with light exercise, and are worse again after heavy exercise. On the other hand, rest and exercise make no consistent changes in patients with psychogenic rheumatism. Patients with fibrositis are benefited by salicylates and have no functional symptoms referable to other organ systems. In contrast, those with psychogenic rheumatism are rarely helped by antirheumatic drugs and their rheumatic complaints are often overshadowed by symptoms referable to other parts of the body. The sedimentation rate and other laboratory tests are normal.

3. Polymyalgia rheumatica

The cause of this condition is uncertain, but the symptoms are striking.[9] Patients are almost invariably elderly. The pain, which is severe, is referred to proximal muscles and other connective tissues, and the erythrocyte sedimentation rate is very rapid, often being 100 mm or more in one hour by the Westergren method. Pain is dramatically controlled by corticosteroids. A distinctive feature that occurs in many patients is giant cell arteritis of the temporal and other cranial arteries.

4. Polymyositis and dermatomyositis

These conditions cause pain and weakness, especially in the proximal muscles of legs and arms. They are distinguished by high serum levels of glutamic or pyruvic transaminases, creatine phosphokinase or aldolase, electromyographic abnormalities, and by muscle biopsy. In many cases only one or two of these tests are positive, so the whole battery of tests may be required for diagnosis. Some 15 to 20 percent of all patients with polymyositis and more than 50 percent of older men with dermatomyositis have occult malignancies.[10] Such malignancies, therefore, should be looked for carefully.

5. Periarthritis of the shoulder and shoulder-hand syndrome

These disorders are discussed in section H of this chapter.

6. Neuropathies

Neuropathies encountered in various entrapment disorders (such as the carpal tunnel syndrome) and in diabetes usually are readily diagnosed by the neurogenic character of the complaints. Diabetes must be excluded in all patients with pain of this type.

F. Arthritis Associated with Features of Serious Connective Tissue Diseases

Systemic lupus has been noted in most of the previous sections of this chapter. Other serious connective tissue diseases, such as progressive systemic sclerosis, dermatomyositis, and polyarteritis nodosa can also mimic rheumatoid arthritis at some phase. In all, the correct diagnosis is made clear by the appearance of other features of the disease in question. A different diagnostic problem is presented by the sudden or gradual appearance of features of one of these diseases during the course of what apparently has been straightforward rheumatoid arthritis. Appreciation of the fact that these transitions or developments can occur should make the physician alert to them. A not uncommon problem in patients with obvious rheumatoid arthritis is the appearance of wrist or foot drop together with superficial areas of cutaneous necrosis. Suitable muscle biopsies reveal arteritis similar to that of polyarteritis nodosa. Whether such lesions are part of rheumatoid disease itself or mark the appearance of a new entity is uncertain.[11]

G. Pain Referable Chiefly to the Back

Back pain is one of the most common problems seen in clinical practice. The more usual causes are as follows:
   □ low back strain or sprain
   □ degenerative disc disease
   □ herniated intervertebral discs
   □ osteophytosis
   □ ankylosing spondylitis
   □ osteoporosis of the spine
   □ other causes

1. Low back strain or sprain
These admittedly vague terms are used here to include the wide variety of mechanical derangements that can result in either acute or chronic lumbar pain, frequently associated with sciatic-like aching in the buttocks and legs. The causes vary from postural abnormalities to acute trauma and congenital defects. Roentgenologic study may reveal loss of the normal lordotic lumbar curve, scoliosis of severe degree, or various congenital defects such as spondylolisthesis or spina bifida. Because similar changes may be seen in patients with no symptoms, the significance of these radiologic abnormalities must be interpreted with caution. Frequently the diagnosis can be merely presumptive because the patient has physical or mechanical abnormality that can cause low back pain, but lacks features that could point to a more specific diagnosis.

2. Degenerative disc disease
Some clinicians would include this condition in the previous category. It is considered separately here for emphasis. Clinically, the symptoms are intermittent attacks of pain in the low back and buttocks, with or without neurogenic referral to the legs. Knee and ankle reflexes are normal. X-rays

showing marked decrease in intervertebral disc space are suggestive but not definitive because similar findings are seen in patients with no pain. Osteophytes are often present, especially at the anterior corners of vertebral bodies adjacent to the degenerated discs. However, it is generally believed that they do not cause pain and are a result of the disc degeneration or are concomitant with it. (See also section G-4 below.)

3. Herniated intervertebral disc

The symptoms are similar to those previously discussed, but they are often more acute and the sciatic pain is more severe. Maneuvers that increase cerebrospinal fluid pressure, such as coughing or straining during defecation, increase the severity of the pain. The diagnosis demands loss or decrease of ankle or knee jerk on the affected side. Definitive diagnosis can be made only if confirmed by a myelographic study.

4. Osteophytosis

This disorder is to the vertebral bodies what osteoarthritis is to the diarthrodial joints. It is commonly found in x-rays, but is rarely a cause of pain, even when the vertebral "beaks" cause partial or complete bridging between two vertebrae. In rare cases, posterior osteophytes encroach on the intervertebral foramina so much that the nerve roots become compressed and cause severe pain in the areas of distribution. Demonstration of such encroachment demands special roentgenologic study.

5. Ankylosing spondylitis

Diagnosis can be uncertain in the early stages before characteristic roentgenologic abnormalities have developed. Suggestive early clinical features are stiffness and aching or pain in the lower back and thighs in a young male whose lumbar spine remains flat on forward bending instead of forming a smooth curve. The knees or, rarely, other peripheral joints may be painful and swollen early in the disease process. Earliest x-ray changes are in the sacroiliac joints, and if these joints are normal six months after the onset of symptoms, the diagnosis is doubtful. Carefully taken oblique views are essential because apparent abnormalities may be erroneously detected in normal sacroiliac joints in conventional flat films of the pelvis. Later, the clinical extension of pain and stiffness to the thoracic region, often with restriction of respiratory motion, and the appearance of the typical syndesmophytes on x-ray study make the diagnosis certain. If ulcerative colitis, regional enteritis, psoriasis, or Reiter's disease is present, sacroiliitis or spondylitis associated with those diseases must be suspect in any patient with lower back pain.[12]

6. Osteoporosis of the spine

Osteoporosis, whether idiopathic or aggravated by rheumatoid arthritis and corticosteroid therapy, is a common cause of back pain, especially in postmenopausal women. When crush fractures are present on x-ray, the diagnosis is clear. However, osteoporosis of the spine can be associated with pain even before the occurrence of fractures. Diagnosis is made probable by the x-ray demonstration of severe osteoporosis with or without crush vertebral fractures.

7. Other causes

Low back pain can be caused by cord or vertebral tumors, infection, Paget's disease, herpes zoster, and other even rarer abnormalities. Such conditions are identified by the course of the disease and special x-ray and laboratory studies.

H. Pain Limited to Shoulders, Neck, and Upper Extremity

Pain in this region so often presents the physician with diagnostic problems that, like pain in the back, it is selected for separate consideration. The various disabilities will be discussed under the following headings:
  □ inflammation or trauma
  □ neurovascular compression at the thoracic outlet
  □ lesions of the cervical spine
  □ reflex neurovascular dystrophy
  □ shoulder pain referred from diseased viscera
  □ fibromyopathies of the shoulder

1. Inflammation or trauma
a. Arthritis

Any type of arthritis may, of course, affect the shoulders. Usually, involvement of other joints indicates the generalized nature of the disease, but diagnosis may be temporarily in doubt when the shoulder is the first joint to be painful. Furthermore, osteoarthritis, usually of the type secondary to an old injury or congenital abnormality, occasionally affects only one shoulder on a chronic basis. In such cases, passive rotation of the shoulder usually is painful and thus helps to distinguish it from extra-articular lesions in tendons and bursa. This maneuver is valid only if the motion is truly passive, and many patients find it difficult not to participate in such movements. Hence, lack of pain on this maneuver is good evidence against intra-articular disease, but, unless the patient has clearly remained passive, the presence of pain does not necessarily indicate arthritis.

b. Tendinitis and bursitis

Probably the most common cause of pain in the shoulder is tendinitis, with or without calcareous deposits, of the supraspinatus tendon. This may occur with or without inflammation of the subdeltoid bursa above the tendon. In acute cases any motion of the arm causes severe pain, which is greatest in the subacromial area, but often radiates up to the occiput and down to the fingers. Tenderness is most exquisite at the lateral portion of the subacromial area at the humeral head and overlying the deltoid muscle. In very acute cases there may be visible swelling and erythema of the shoulder. In subacute and chronic cases there often is a history of a previous acute attack. The symptoms are similar to, but less severe than, those of acute cases.Abduction and external rotation are the most painful movements. An x-ray may show calcareous deposits in the line of the supraspinatus tendon or in other rotator tendons implicated in the individual patient. If calcium has ruptured into the subdeltoid bursa, this may appear on x-ray examination.

c. Bicipital tenosynovitis
Acute inflammation of the biceps tendon and its sheath is fairly common. Although probably always secondary to trauma, the trauma may be so minor that it escaped notice. Pain at the shoulder radiates down the biceps muscle, often to the forearm, and is exaggerated by abduction and internal rotation. The tenderness is greatest overlying the bicipital groove.

d. Rotator cuff lesions
This term usually is limited to complete or partial tears of one of the rotator tendons or of the mesh-like connective tissue cuff that connects them. A complete rupture of the supraspinatus tendon is associated with trauma, sudden pain, and inability to raise or rotate the arm. A snap-like sensation or a sulcus at the point of the tear often occurs. In elderly people, a similar tear may occur in the biceps tendon.

e. Adhesive capsulitis
The so-called "frozen shoulder" is thought to be initiated by trauma, often trivial, to the shoulder. The course is one of gradual onset of pain similar to that of bicipital tendinitis, becoming more severe and leading to loss of motion at the scapulo-humeral joint so that the only shoulder motion is that of the scapula.

2. Neurovascular compression at the thoracic outlet
Various mechanisms, usually based on congenital or developmental abnormalities of bony structures or insertions of muscles, may cause pressure on the brachial plexus and accompanying vessels as they traverse the thoracic outlet between the clavicle and subclavius muscle, or between the scalenus anticus muscle and the first rib. Such abnormal pressure can occur in patients with cervical rib, scalenus anticus syndrome, costoclavicular syndrome, and the hyperabduction syndrome. In all of these conditions, the patient has an aching pain of neuralgic character in the shoulder and arm, coldness and numbness of the hand with discoloration, and lessened blood pressure in the affected arm. The symptoms increase as the arm is moved.

A cervical rib may occur without symptoms, but is demonstrated by x-ray examination. The costoclavicular syndrome is exaggerated by downward and backward strain on the shoulders, as when carrying a heavy backpack. The hyperabduction syndrome is exaggerated by laterally circumducting the arms and clasping the hands over the head. The symptoms due to cervical rib and pressure by the scalenus muscles are exaggerated by the Adson maneuver: marked decrease in palpable pulse when the patient takes a deep breath, hyperextends his neck, and rotates his head to the affected side. Numbness may also be caused by prolonged downward pull as when carrying a heavy suitcase.

3. Lesions of the cervical spine

These include radiculitis resulting from degenerative disc disease, foraminal osteophytes, herniation of the nucleus pulposus, and space-occupying lesions of the spinal cord. All cause aching in the shoulder area and often in the neck and arm. This aching tends to be increased by motion of the neck. X-ray examination in the lateral view shows straightening of the normal cervical curve, probably due to muscle spasm, and thinning of one or more intervertebral discs. Oblique views may show encroachment on intervertebral foramina by osteophytes. Unless myelographic study is indicated, herniation of the nucleus pulposus and space-occupying lesions of the cord may not show any abnormality by x-ray except straightening of the cervical curve.

4. Reflex neurovascular dystrophy

The shoulder-hand syndrome may start with either shoulder or hand involvement, but within several weeks both usually are affected. At onset there is stiffness and soreness or severe pain in the shoulder or hand followed by swelling, vasomotor changes, and hyperesthesia of the hand. After a period of months, the pain and swelling disappear, leaving atrophy of the skin and muscles of the hand with beginning contractures of the fingers. In later stages, the dystrophic changes of the skin and soft tissue of the hands and lower arm continue with more advanced contractures and marked limitation of motion of the shoulder, frequently progressing to "frozen shoulder." After the initial phase, x-rays show spotty demineralization of the head of the humerus, carpal bones, and phalanges. Later, this demineralization may be diffuse. In the early stages, rheumatoid arthritis may be suspected, especially when both arms are affected. Even then, however, the diffuse character of the symptoms points to the correct diagnosis, since the pain, swelling, and tenderness occur throughout the hand and fingers instead of being limited to the joints. Patients frequently have a history of recent catastrophic illness, such as myocardial infarction or hemiplegia on the involved side. Other common preceding disorders are trauma to the neck or shoulder, cervical disc degeneration, and foraminal osteophytosis.

5. Shoulder pain referred from diseased viscera

Pain in the shoulder, neck, and upper arm may occur in patients with myocardial infarction, biliary tract disease, and lesions causing diaphragmatic irritation. These visceral diseases must, therefore, be borne in mind when other causes of shoulder pain are not apparent.

6. Fibromyopathies of the shoulder

Vague pain in the shoulder, in the absence of other more specific causes and with normal erythrocyte sedimentation rate, may warrant the equally vague diagnosis of fibrositis. (See section E-1, page 26.)

I. Elbow, Wrist, and Hand Problems

In addition to arthritis affecting the joints of the forearm and hand, there are common, painful nonarticular difficulties that require recognition for proper and effective treatment. They include the following:
  □ tennis elbow
  □ olecranon bursitis
  □ carpal tunnel syndrome
  □ DeQuervain's disease
  ⊔ ganglion
  □ "trigger finger" and "snapping thumb"
  □ Dupuytren's contracture

1. Tennis elbow or epicondylitis

This term has been applied to any strain of the muscle attachments at the lateral epicondyle of the elbow, whether or not it results from tennis. Bursitis may be present. It is nearly always caused by trauma. Differential diagnostic clues are that elbow joint motion is painless and full and no swelling is noted, but there is localized tenderness over the external epicondyle or radiohumeral joint. Supination of the forearm against resistance is painful.

2. Olecranon bursitis

Swelling, fluctuation, and tenderness at the point of the elbow characterize this condition. It may result from trauma, rheumatoid arthritis (nodules may be found in the bursa), gout (tophus in the bursa), or, occasionally, sepsis (usually resulting from a break in overlying skin). Fluid should be aspirated for diagnosis. (See synovial fluid analysis, Chapter 3.)

3. Carpal tunnel syndrome

Possible causes are trauma, rheumatoid arthritis, myxedema, and amyloidosis. The most frequent precipitating events are occupational strains on the tendons. Compression of the median nerve as it passes under the volar carpal ligament with the flexor tendons of the fingers thickens the tendon sheaths, producing numbness and tingling, which is most severe at night, in the second, third, and fourth fingers. Tapping the wrist on the volar surface may elicit the tingling (Tinel's sign). Holding the wrist in acute flexion for a minute may also produce the tingling (Phelan's sign). Nerve conduction tests of the median nerve help to prove the diagnosis. Atrophy of the thenar muscles develops as the condition persists.

4. DeQuervain's disease
This disorder is stenosing tenosynovitis of the conjoined tendons of the long abductor and short extensor of the thumb as they cross the radial styloid at the wrist. The most common cause is occupational trauma. Tenderness at the radial styloid may be present. The diagnosis is confirmed by flexing the thumb into the palm with the other fingers flexed over the thumb and rotating the hand in an ulnar direction at the wrist. This procedure, Finkelstein's test, produces sharp pain in DeQuervain's disease.

5. Ganglion
Hygromatous bursae may develop on either the volar or dorsal surface of the wrist from trauma, rheumatoid synovitis, or, rarely, from gout or sepsis (e.g., gonococcal or tuberculous infection). Passive movement of the wrist is full and relatively painless, but active flexion or extension of the fingers may produce pain or cause "bunching" of the swelling, which is fluctuant or tense.

6. "Trigger finger" and "snapping thumb"
These conditions are forms of digital flexor tenosynovitis. They usually result from repeated hard grasping and may be complications of rheumatoid arthritis or degenerative joint disease. Rarely, they occur with septic conditions, such as tuberculous arthritis. Passive flexion and extension of the affected fingers or thumb may be normal, but active flexion, particularly against resistance, elicits pain and may lock the digit in flexion, requiring release by passive manipulation. Swelling along the tendon sheath may be noted, and crepitation may be felt along the sheath with active flexion and extension.

7. Dupuytren's contracture
This idiopathic contracture of the palmar fascia may present with nodules in the distal palm over the fourth flexor tendon (sometimes extending to the third and fifth) leading to flexion deformity of the affected finger. The firm, puckered thickening prevents full extension, but flexion is unimpaired.

J. Leg and Foot Problems

Nonarticular disorders of the lower extremity are frequent, painful, and often persistent. For proper treatment, they must be differentiated from arthritis of the hip, knee, ankle, or foot. The more common afflictions are as follows:

- □ trochanteric bursitis
- □ sciatica
- □ prepatellar bursitis
- □ patellar chondromalacea
- □ cartilage derangements of the knee
- □ tendinitis of the ankle or instep
- □ calcaneal bursitis
- □ footstrain and flat foot
- □ bunion
- □ "hammer toes"

1. Trochanteric bursitis

This condition, usually traumatic, can be differentiated from hip joint disease by the absence of pain on passive rotation of the flexed hip and by the presence of localized tenderness behind and sometimes slightly above the trochanter of the hip. X-rays may show some calcific deposit in the bursa rather than changes in the hip joint.

2. Sciatica

Sciatica neuritis produces an aching pain down the posterior thigh, with sharp pain induced in the lower back by flexion of the hip with the knee straight (Lasegue's sign). The cause is usually a degenerative change in the lower lumbar spine. X-rays are often helpful in diagnosis.

3. Prepatellar bursitis

"Housemaid's knee" or "nun's knee" results from frequent kneeling on hard surfaces. Tenderness, swelling, and fluctuation are noted anterior and immediately inferior to the patella. Knee flexion and extension are normal.

4. Patellar chondromalacea

Painful knees in young people, which worsen when walking or kneeling, with palpable (or even audible) crepitation of the patella against the femur, suggests this diagnosis. X-rays are seldom helpful in diagnosis until late stages of this developmental disorder.

5. Cartilage derangements of the knee

Tears of the semilunar cartilages of the knee are particularly common from athletic injuries. "Locking" of the knee in flexion and painful effusion are suggestive. McMurray's sign—pain on attempted extension of the acutely flexed knee held either in internal or external rotation from the ankle—may be positive. Orthopedic consultation is advisable.

6. Tendinitis of the ankle or instep

This condition is differentiated from ankle joint involvement by local tenderness along the extensor or flexor tendons and an absence of pain on passive flexion or extension of the ankle. However, flexing and extending the toes actively produce pain. Tarsal tunnel syndrome may result if the tendon sheath swelling is sufficient to cause pressure on the nerves as they pass together under the retinaculum.

7. Calcaneal bursitis

Tenderness and sometimes swelling over the insertion of the Achilles tendon to the calcaneus ("soldier's heel") or tenderness under the heel at the insertion of the plantar fascia are clues to diagnosis of this usually traumatic condition. X-rays may show spurs at the attachments to the calcaneus.

8. Footstrain and flat foot

Painful flat feet, with maximum tenderness under the long arch (instep) and pronation, require arch supports or surgical consultation. Calluses under the metatarsal heads are frequent.

9. Bunion

Bursitis over the medial surface of the first metatarsal phalangeal joint often accompanies hallux valgus (lateral deviation) of the great toe.

10. "Hammer toes"

Contracture of the toes in a "cockup" position may result from tendon shortening, badly fitting short shoes, or from rheumatoid arthritic subluxation of the metatarsophalangeal joints. Corns over the affected toes and callosities under the metatarsophalangeal joints are common.

K. Arthritis in Children

Essentially, all forms of rheumatic disease which affect adults can also affect children, the obvious exception being osteoarthritis and other degenerative processes peculiar to older age. The most common diseases that are especially prone to affect children are the following:
   □ rheumatic fever
   □ juvenile rheumatoid arthritis
   □ pyogenic arthritis and osteomyelitis
   □ tuberculous arthritis
   □ leukemia
   □ anaphylactoid purpura
   □ foreign protein reactions
   □ systemic lupus erythematosus
   □ rubella arthritis

- □ erythema nodosum
- □ sickle cell disease
- □ hemophilia
- □ slipped femoral epiphysis
- □ Perthe's disease
- □ congenital syphilis
- □ child beating

1. Rheumatic fever

The diagnostic features in adults noted in section A-1 apply also to children. In very young children, however, joint involvement may be absent. In patients with fever and debility, the appearance of carditis, erythema marginatum, or typical small rheumatic subcutaneous nodules over bony prominences of elbows, ankles, knees, knuckles, and cranium makes the diagnosis clear. A rising antistreptolysin titer is suggestive but not diagnostic.

2. Juvenile rheumatoid arthritis

There are three general types of this disease: cases with multiple joint involvement similar to rheumatoid arthritis in adults, pauciarticular cases with involvement of only one to three joints, and cases of the type originally described by Still with little or no arthritis but with high fever and other systemic manifestations. The first type is diagnosed using the same criteria as in adults, except that tests for rheumatoid factors usually are negative and subcutaneous nodules, when present, more nearly resemble the small nodules of rheumatic fever than the larger ones of adult rheumatoid arthritis.

Pauciarticular cases resemble the former type, except for the small number of joints affected and the comparatively benign nature of articular damage. Whereas iritis can occur in any patient with rheumatoid arthritis, it is especially common and severe in children with the pauciarticular form of disease.

The acute, systemic form of juvenile rheumatoid arthritis is often thought to be rheumatic fever at first because of its acuteness, fever, and systemic features (which may include carditis). Fever may be higher than in rheumatic fever and tends to be more spiking in character. A fairly characteristic evanescent, macular rash may be present. This rash lacks the marginate outline of erythema marginatum seen in rheumatic fever.

In all forms, the erythrocyte sedimentation rate is high, though less so in pauciarticular cases. Antistreptolysin titers are low unless there has been coincidental recent hemolytic streptococcal infection. Tests for rheumatoid factors usually are negative. X-ray study reveals only soft-tissue swelling in the early phases of disease and, subsequently, articular damage paralleling the clinical state of the joints. In some patients the radiologic demonstration of sacroiliac damage has raised the question of whether these patients may not actually have juvenile ankylosing spondylitis.

It must be noted that young children with rheumatoid arthritis often make little complaint of joint pain, and limping or clumsy use of an arm may lead the parent to examine the child and discover joint swelling.

3. Pyogenic arthritis and osteomyelitis

Pyogenic arthritis in the child is similar to that in the adult. Occasionally pyogenic osteomyelitis close to a joint may lead to articular pain, tenderness, and effusion. When the culture is sterile the diagnosis may be obscure. However, fever of septic type, localized tenderness, and x-ray study help disclose the true nature of the illness.

4. Tuberculous arthritis

This disorder resembles that in adults. (See section B-5, page 20).

5. Leukemia

Articular features of leukemias are more often encountered in children than in adults, and may mimic rheumatic fever until hematologic study makes the diagnosis obvious. Bone pain on weight bearing is often a prominent symptom.

6. Anaphylactoid purpura

This disorder is more often seen in children and young teenagers than in adults. When purpura is apparent the diagnosis is quickly made. However, if purpura is delayed, the combination of fever and articular and abdominal pain may suggest rheumatic fever. If renal involvement also is present, systemic lupus may be suspected. With the development of purpura, and in the absence of laboratory indices of lupus, the correct diagnosis becomes apparent.

7. Foreign protein reactions (serum sickness type)
8. Systemic lupus erythematosus
9. Rubella arthritis
10. Erythema nodosum

These conditions have the same features that characterize them in adults, as discussed earlier in this chapter. Indeed, rubella arthritis and erythema nodosum are more frequently seen in children than in adults.

11. Sickle cell disease
12. Hemophilia

Peripheral arthritis of acute onset is frequently observed in patients with these hematologic diseases. The nature of the arthritis is made clear by recognition of the underlying cause.

13. Slipped femoral epiphysis

The usual site of this abnormality is the head of the femur. The child resists weight bearing and lies with his leg in external rotation to avoid internal rotation. The hip goes into external rotation when it is flexed passively. Roentgenologic examination reveals the abnormal position of the femoral head at the epiphysis.

14. Perthe's disease

This form of avascular necrosis of the femoral head in children is associated with gradually increasing discomfort on weight bearing and motion. The pain often radiates to the knee and motion of the hip is limited. Diagnosis is made on x-ray demonstration of flattening of the femoral head and the characteristic motling of avascular necrosis.

15. Congenital syphilis

The so-called Clutton's joint of late congenital syphilis is rarely seen today. The knees are most commonly involved, but other joints may be affected. The course is one of chronic synovial effusion without erythema and with little pain and local warmth. The diagnosis usually is not suspected until a positive serologic test is reported and is confirmed by prompt response to antiluetic therapy.

16. Child beating

Small children who have been repeatedly struck over the knuckles with a ruler or similar object may develop swelling, pain, tenderness, and limitation of motion simulating juvenile rheumatoid arthritis. Diagnosis is suggested by an inapporpriate attitude on the part of the parents or babysitter, and is confirmed by x-ray examination revealing periosteal proliferation and tiny spicules of bone in the soft tissues.

REFERENCES

1. Ehrlich, G. E.: Intermittent and periodic arthritic syndromes. In Arthritis and Allied Conditions, *ed. J. L. Hollander and D. J. McCarty, Jr., 8th edition, Philadelphia, Lea & Febiger, 1972, pp. 821-831.*
2. McCarty, D. J., Jr., Kohn, N. N., and Faires, J. S.: The significance of calcium phosphate crystals in the synovial fluid of arthritic patients: the "pseudogout syndrome," Ann. Intern. Med. 56:711, May 1962.
3. McEwen, C.: Arthritis accompanying ulcerative colitis, Clin. Orthop. 57:9, March-April 1968.
4. Schmid, F. R.: Unusual features and special types of infectious arthritis. In Arthritis and Allied Conditions, *ed. J. L. Hollander and D. J. McCarty, Jr., 8th edition, Philadelphia, Lea & Febiger, 1972, pp. 1274-1276.*
5. Shulman, L. E. and Harvey, A. M.: Polyarteritis and other arteritic syndromes. In Arthritis and Allied Conditions, *ed. J. L. Hollander and D. J. McCarty, Jr., 8th edition, Philadelphia, Lea & Febiger, 1972, p. 934.*
6. Spilberg, I., Siltzbach, L. E., and McEwen, C.: The arthritis of sarcoidosis, Arthritis Rheum. 12:126, April 1969.

7. Vaughan, J. H.: The rheumatoid factors. In Arthritis and Allied Conditions, *ed. J. L. Hollander and D. J. McCarty, Jr., 8th edition, Philadelphia, Lea & Febiger, 1972, p. 165.*

8. McEwen, C.: Osteoarthritis of the fingers with ankylosis, Arthritis Rheum. 11:734, December 1968.

9. Wilske, K. R. and Healey, L. A.: Polymyalgia rheumatica: a manifestation of systemic giant-cell arteritis, Ann. Intern. Med. 66:77, January 1967.

10. Pearson, C. M.: Polymyositis and dermatomyositis. In Arthritis and Allied Conditions, *ed. J. L. Hollander and D. J. McCarty, Jr., 8th edition, Philadelphia, Lea & Febiger, 1972, p. 948.*

11. Schmid, F. R., Cooper, N. S., Ziff, M., and McEwen, C.: Arteritis in rheumatoid arthritis, Amer. J. Med. 30:56, January 1961.

12. McEwen, C. et al.: Ankylosing spondylitis and spondylitis accompanying ulcerative colitis, regional enteritis, psoriasis and Reiter's disease: a comparative study, Arthritis Rheum. 14:291, May-June 1971.

CHAPTER 3

A Practical Guide to Special Tests and Diagnostic Procedures in Arthritis

Alan S. Cohen, M.D., F.A.C.P.

Conrad Wesselhoeft Professor of Medicine
Boston University School of Medicine
Boston, Massachusetts

Chief of Medicine and Director
Thorndike Memorial Laboratories
Boston City Hospital

Head, Section on Arthritis and Connective Tissue Diseases
Boston University Medical Center

CHAPTER 3

A Practical Guide to
Special Tests and
Diagnostic Procedures
in Arthritis

Alan S. Cohen, M.D., F.A.C.P.

A wide variety of laboratory procedures are available for the clinician to use in his diagnostic evaluation of patients with articular diseases. Each has unique value in assisting the physician toward a total assessment of the patient, although few, if any, have absolute specificity for one disease. Many of these tests have been reviewed recently in great detail.[1,2] The purpose of the present review is to discuss the procedures most likely to be of diagnostic assistance.

A. The Joint Space and Arthrocentesis

The joint space is a part of the connective tissue of the body. As such, it may reflect not only local abnormalities but generalized inflammatory or metabolic disease. The lining membrane differs from others in the body in its discontinuous nature and by the presence of a thin layer of synovial cells, variously described as resembling fibroblasts, macrophages, or both. The synovial fluid in the space is clear and viscous and differs from serous cavity fluids (which are plasma ultrafiltrates) and cerebrospinal fluid (which is essentially a secretory product of the choroid plexus). Though joint fluid is in part dialysate, its one major unusual component, hyaluronic acid, is secreted locally, probably by lining cells. Since it is a high-molecular-weight polyelectrolyte that is asymmetrical and long-chained, it contributes not only to the physicochemical makeup of synovial fluid, but in part determines what enters this space.

The majority of patients who present with an acute arthritis will have an acutely swollen joint. In such a patient with undiagnosed articular disease and an associated joint effusion, examination of the synovial fluid is mandatory. The general approach to the joint (most frequently the knee) is through the extensor surface, where major blood vessels and nerves are sparse and the synovial pouch is more superficial. If the synovial fluid sugar is to be measured, the patient should have fasted for at least six hours. Careful skin preparation at the aspiration site with surgical detergent, iodine, and alcohol helps preclude infection, the one rare but serious complication of arthrocentesis. The needle should be at least 20 gauge. After appropriate skin antisepsis and intracutaneous instillation of one to two percent procaine or lidocaine, the aspirating needle is inserted through skin and subcutaneous tissue. It meets a small degree of resistance when it reaches the capsule and finally passes easily into the joint cavity. While minimal amounts of fluid will suffice for the basic studies needed, as a rule 10 to 15 ml will allow extensive laboratory testing. The recommended tests, amounts of synovial fluid needed, and anticoagulant are listed in Table 1. (See also Chapter 7.)

B. Synovial Fluid

1. General features
Normal synovial fluid is clear, yellow, viscous, and does not clot. In patients with inflammatory joint disease the appearance of the fluid varies with the severity and duration of effusion. In general, when the membrane is more acutely inflamed, the fluid becomes increasingly cloudy and less viscous and it tends to clot. The cloudiness is caused by increased numbers of white blood cells and other debris that appear in association with the inflammatory process. The change in viscosity is due to an alteration in the physicochemical state of the hyaluronate-protein complex in the synovial fluid, and the clot is caused by the appearance of larger molecules, including various blood-clotting factors, in synovial fluid. These larger molecules appear because of the increased permeability of the synovial membrane.

2. Culture
Routine bacteriologic cultures should be carried out on *all* synovial fluids, preferably at the time of arthrocentesis. A general medium such as trypticase soy broth may be used or, if there is any possibility of a gonococcal infection, chocolate agar or its equivalent should be used for culture at the bedside. Appropriate cultures and guinea pig inoculation should be performed if tuberculosis is suspected. These precautions, even in studying

Procedure	Anticoagulant	Amount of Synovial Fluid (in ml)

Culture
  Aerobic
  Anaerobic
  Guinea pig inoculation
  where indicated
	Sterile tube with 1 to 2 drops of heparin	2-5

Cytology White blood count, differential, crystals, inclusions	EDTA (5 mg) or heparin (1 to 2 drops)	2-5
Analysis of clot, hyaluronate (mucin), general appearance, crystals, and inclusions	None	2-5
Sugar	Potassium oxalate	3-5

TABLE 1
Synovial Fluid Collection

a "routine" effusion in a patient with rheumatoid arthritis, are quite important, because damaged joints may be unsuspected sites of superimposed infection, and a significant morbidity and mortality has been reported. In an acutely inflamed joint this procedure is particularly important. Smear of the fluid and gram stain is also useful but must be interpreted with caution, because clumps of hyaluronate-protein have occasionally been confused with bacteria.

3. Cytology

The tube containing anticoagulant and synovial fluid is shaken for one or two minutes until they are thoroughly mixed. A white cell count is performed in the same manner as the procedure for peripheral blood. The one important difference is that a hypotonic (0.3 percent) saline diluent with added methylene blue to aid in cell differentiation is used instead of acid diluent. Acid would precipitate the hyaluronate and significantly alter the count. Smears are made and examined after Wright's stain has been added.

Normal synovial fluid is quite acellular, containing fewer than 200 cells per mm^3, and has a low (about 25 percent) polymorphonuclear white cell count. Joint effusions in patients with various diseases can usually be designated inflammatory if the synovial fluid white cells and polymorphonuclear cells are increased, or noninflammatory if there is little or no increase in the white cell and polymorphonuclear count (see Table 2). In acute infections, the total count is almost invariably elevated. In our series, the mean was 73,000 cells per mm^3, but greater and lesser figures have been reported. Polymorphonuclear cells usually account for more than 90 percent of the total count.

Recent studies have revealed other aspects of synovial fluid cytology that are very important in differential diagnosis of acute and chronic arthritis.[3-6] A drop of fresh synovial fluid, or a well-mixed drop of fluid prepared as described above and refrigerated, is placed on a clean microscopic slide, covered with a clean cover slip, and observed under a microscope. In osteoarthritis the number of cells will be small, but fairly numerous irregular shards of cartilage will be noted, resulting from the desquamation of small bits of cartilage from the joint surface. Occasionally, these shards of cartilage may be noted in traumatic arthritis fluids that are not very bloody, or in pseudogout, where the bits of cartilage may contain crystals of calcium pyrophosphate. However, the finding of numerous bits of cartilage debris is strongly suggestive of degenerative joint disease.

In several forms of arthritis the polymorphonuclear leukocytes may contain cytoplasmic inclusions. When an unstained, wet specimen is viewed under regular light, these inclusions appear as dark globular areas in the cytoplasm, which are larger than the usual cellular granules. Such cells are seen in small numbers in any form of arthritis in which phagocytosis is occurring in the joint space, but they are much more numerous in proportion to the total cell population in rheumatoid arthritis and septic arthritis. It was initially hoped that there might be diagnostic aid from finding such cells in rheumatoid arthritis fluids, but while the large proportion of such inclusion-bearing cells may be suggestive of rheumatoid arthritis, they may be observed (usually in lesser numbers) in other disease states, and inclusions other than rheumatoid factors (i.e., fibrin and other debris) may be identified.

The search for crystals in wet preparations of synovial fluid may yield more specific diagnostic aid than any other tests. Needle-like crystals of monosodium urate may be seen under regular light if the condenser is turned down. They may be free in the fluid, but in acute gout they are mostly within the polymorphonuclear leukocytes. If polarizing disks are placed in the eyepiece and condenser of a regular microscope and rotated until they cross (darkest background), the crystals show up as bright needles against the dark background. They are best identified under a polarizing microscope with a red plate compensator in place. This gives a red background, with crystals showing up as yellow needles when parallel to the plane of the compensator, and blue when viewed at right angles (negatively birefringent). Many bits of crystal may be seen within the cells, and often large crystals will be seen apparently projecting through white blood cells.

Group	Disease	Appearance	Viscosity	Mucin Clot	WBC Count (avg./mm³)	Percent Polys	Special Findings
Group I	Normal	Clear, yellow	High	Good	>200	>10	
	Traumatic Arthritis	Straw to red Clear to cloudy	High	Good	>2000 (many RBC)	>25	Cartilage fragments (few)
	Osteo-arthritis	Yellow Clear	High	Good	1000	>25	Cartilage fragments (many)
Group II Inflammatory	Systemic Lupus Erythematosus	Slightly cloudy	High	Good	3000	20	Lupus erythematosus cells (Wright Stained Smear)
	Rheumatic Fever	Slightly cloudy	Decreased	Good	10,000	>50	Few inclusion body cells
	Reiter's Disease	Cloudy	Decreased	Fair	15,000	>60	Complement often increased Polys in macrophages (?)
	Pseudogout	Cloudy if acute	Decreased	Fair	>10,000	>50	Rhomboid, positively birefringent. Crystals (Ca Pyrophosphate) in cells or cartilage fragments
	Gouty Arthritis	Cloudy	Decreased	Fair-poor	13,500	>70	Needle-like negatively birefringent. Crystals, free or in cells (monosodium urate)
	Rheumatoid Arthritis (active)	Greenish Cloudy	Low	Fair-poor	15,500	>70	Many cells contain large cytoplasmic inclusions Complement low. Latex +
Group III Septic	Tuberculous Arthritis	Cloudy	Low	Poor	25,000	50	AFB may be in smear. Glucose lowered. Culture may be +
	Septic Arthritis (acute)	Turbid to purulent	Low	Poor	>75,000	>90	Glucose much lower than in blood. Culture positive. Complement low (?)

TABLE 2
Synovial Fluid Analysis

In articular chondrocalcinosis, and particularly in pseudogout, the fluid will contain crystals, either rhomboid or rod-shaped. Such crystals may be free in the fluid, but are more often seen in the bits of cartilage or in the cytoplasm of the leukocytes. They may be seen through polarizing disks in a regular microscope, but are most easily identified under compensated polarized light. They appear as weakly positively birefringent crystals of varying size and shape.

The identification of crystals, particularly in significant numbers within cells, is pathognomonic of crystal-induced synovitis, either from urate (gout) or from calcium pyrophosphate (pseudogout). Rarely, in chronic effusions from rheumatoid arthritis, the typical, plate-like crystals of cholesterol, with notched corners, may be noted. If the joint has been recently injected with corticosteroid, the aspirated fluid will contain numerous crystals of the injected steroid, which must not be confused with crystal-induced synovitis.

4. Mucin test for synovial fluid hyaluronate

Hyaluronic acid, a mucopolysaccharide of high molecular weight, is responsible for the viscosity of the synovial fluid. A simple mucin test is one of a battery of tests to determine whether an effusion is inflammatory. The test is conducted by diluting one ml of joint fluid with four ml of two percent acetic acid and mixing the resulting solution. If the mucin is normal, a tight ropy mass forms in a clear solution. This is termed a "good" mucin. A softer mass with shreds is a "fair" mucin, while a "poor" mucin shows shreds and soft small masses in a turbid solution. A "very poor" mucin is one that demonstrates only a few flecks in a very cloudy solution. In acute infections the mucin clot is usually "poor," and in the inflammatory forms of arthritis the clot is "fair" to "poor." It is "good" in osteoarthritis.

5. Synovial fluid proteins

Under normal conditions, the total synovial fluid protein is about one-quarter that of the blood. Numerous studies have been performed to determine whether specific fractions might be related to specific disease states, but the findings have not been promising. One may conclude that if the synovial fluid total protein is over 2.5 g per 100 ml the fluid is not normal, and if it is over 4.5 g per 100 ml there is significant inflammation.

Rheumatoid factors may be found in synovial fluid in titers comparable to or slightly lower than in serum, and in rare instances they may be present in synovial fluid and absent from serum. Antinuclear antibodies may also be found in synovial fluid, and complement has been shown to be decreased in rheumatoid and lupus effusions.

6. Miscellaneous findings

Synovial fluid normally contains little lipid, but rheumatoid effusions show an increased lipid content. The content of various enzymes also is increased in inflamed joints, but again this finding is not specific for rheumatoid arthritis. The glucose content of synovial fluid, which normally approximates that of serum, is markedly diminished in the presence of infection and may show a modest decrease (10 to 30 mg per 100 ml) in rheumatoid effusions.

C. Nonspecific Abnormalities of Blood and Serum

Abnormal routine blood tests in a patient with rheumatic disease, while secondary in diagnostic significance to clinical findings and of less immediate relevance than synovial fluid changes, offer an additional index that may be of value in a particular patient. Certain of these tests have further importance in the formulation of concepts of pathogenesis, and have also been of value in epidemiologic studies. These laboratory procedures may be divided into two groups. First are those that reflect the presence of the inflammatory process; they have little diagnostic specificity, but are of value in estimating the severity of the disease process and in following its course in a particular patient. In the second group are certain serologic tests that are of greater diagnostic value.

1. Red blood cells, white blood cells, and serum proteins

Anemia, most often hypochromic, was found in about 20 percent of a large series of cases of rheumatoid arthritis.[7] It was apparently related to disease activity and to total severity of involvement. Leukocytosis also occurred in 20 percent of the patients and was sometimes associated with an acute onset of clinical disease. Lesser percentages of patients had granulocytosis, eosinophilia, and lymphocytosis. Leukopenia was unusual and was seen only in patients with severe disease of long duration. Abnormalities of the serum proteins on routine electrophoresis are frequently seen in rheumatoid arthritis,[8] but no good correlation with clinical findings or the course of the disease has been established.

2. Erythrocyte sedimentation rate (ESR)

As a consequence of synovial or systemic inflammation in active rheumatoid arthritis, acute phase phenomena are almost invariably present. Of these, the most valuable is the Westergren erythrocyte sedimentation rate.[9] This test is performed by collecting two ml venous blood in 0.5 ml of 3.8 percent sodium citrate, drawing the blood up to the 200-mm mark in a Westergren tube (2.5 mm in internal diameter), allowing the tube to stand vertically for an hour at room temperature, and then measuring the fall in the red cell column in mm.[10]

Cohen

Normal values are one to three mm fall in one hour for males, and four to seven for females. This test is nonspecific, and will be abnormal in many conditions associated with acute or chronic inflammation, ranging from acute myocardial infarction to chronic tuberculosis. (An additional source of confusion in interpretation is presented by a recent report of elevated erythrocyte sedimentation rates in a percentage of women taking oral contraceptive drugs.) Abnormal elevation of the erythrocyte sedimentation rate is mediated, at least in part, by an increase in plasma fibrinogen and immunoglobulins. Elevated values are found in almost all patients with active rheumatoid arthritis. A normal erythrocyte sedimentation rate in a patient in whom the diagnosis of rheumatoid arthritis is being considered should lead to a careful re-evaluation. In this limited sense, the erythrocyte sedimentation rate, in spite of its nonspecificity, may be said to have a certain diagnostic value. Obviously, its major value is in estimating the severity of the disease process and in following the course over a period of time.

Other methods of measuring the erythrocyte sedimentation rate include the Wintrobe technique, which is widely used but is significantly less sensitive and accurate. No obvious advantages compensate for the technical difficulties of the Rourke-Ernsterne and Cutler methods. Among other tests for acute phase phenomena, C-reactive protein[11] is positive in the majority of patients with active rheumatoid arthritis, and may be detected by the use of specific antisera.

D. Uric Acid

Uric acid is the final product of purine metabolism in man and is formed by the action of the enzyme xanthine oxidase on xanthine and hypoxanthine. The miscible pool of uric acid, as determined by radioactive isotopes, is approximately 1200 mg. This is formed from exogenous dietary purines and from endogenous sources. It has been amply demonstrated that uric acid is primarily formed from glycine and other simple precursors in the body.[12] If no purine is taken exogenously, there is only a slight reduction in the pool and in the serum uric acid.

Although the biosynthetic pathways for purines have been elaborately worked out, the specific metabolic abnormality or abnormalities in primary gout are still to be determined. In uric acid overproducers several factors have been considered: a defect in the feedback control of purine biosynthesis, abnormalities in glutamine metabolism, and, more recently, structural mutants of the enzyme hypoxanthine-guanine phosphoribosyltransferase (HG-PRTase) with decreased activity[13,14] and structural mutants of phosphoribosylpyrophosphate (PP-ribose-P) synthetase with increased activity.[15]

52

The normal turnover of uric acid is roughly 700 mg in 24 hours. In the kidney, uric acid is thought to be filtered completely, and under normal circumstances it is completely reabsorbed. Recent evidence suggests that tubular secretion of uric acid takes place locally in the kidney. The urinary output in the normal person is usually under 500 mg in 24 hours. The remainder of the uric acid is excreted into the gastrointestinal tract where it is degraded by uricolysis by the bacterial flora. Fecal excretion is practically nonexistent.

In 1848, Garrod demonstrated the presence of hyperuricemia in gouty patients.[16] This discovery has been regarded as a historical landmark in medicine. Normally, the concentration of uric acid in adult males is approximately seven mg per 100 ml (enzymatic determination). In females, it is about one mg lower.[13,17] The measurement varies from one laboratory to the next, depending on the methodology used.[13]

A detailed description of the many factors contributing to the uric acid level is beyond the scope of this discussion. Genetic factors, metabolic factors, and drug effects on the kidney all play a role. There is no question that the deposition of crystalline monosodium urate monohydrate crystals is primary in the genesis of an acute attack of gout. It is equally clear that we cannot diagnose acute gout on the basis of hyperuricemia alone, even when associated with acute arthritis, because other diseases may mimic acute gout. The presence of hyperuricemia, however, should lead to a thorough evaluation for gout, including wherever possible synovial fluid analysis for the crystals by polarization microscopy.

Secondary gout is seen in disorders with accelerated nucleoprotein turnover (i.e., leukemia, myeloid metaplasia) or interference with renal handling of uric acid by drugs (i.e., thiazides) or due to intrinsic renal disease. Thus the evaluation for the significance of hyperuricemia includes a careful family and drug history, physical examination with particular attention to the joints and presence or absence of nodules or tophi, examination of synovial fluid, serologic tests, and occasionally a trial of colchicine if acute arthritis is present.

E. Rheumatoid factors (RFs)

Rheumatoid factors are found in the sera of 70 to 80 percent of patients with definite or classical rheumatoid arthritis.[18] They are 19S immunoglobulins (IgM) and will react, in serologic systems, with 7S immunoglobulins (IgG). It should be appreciated that IgG may have a dual immunologic character in tests for rheumatoid factors acting as antibody in reaction with antigens, such as red blood cells, and as an antigen in the reaction with rheumatoid factors. Consequently, rheumatoid factors are sometimes classified as "anti-antibody." Human rheumatoid factors will react not only with autologous and other human IgG, but also with those from the rabbit and other species. While previously there was some doubt as to whether the reaction of rheumatoid factors with gamma globulin was an immune process, it is now generally accepted that rheumatoid factors are indeed antibodies.[19] Apparent synthesis of rheumatoid factors by plasma cells in synovial tissue and in lymph nodes from patients with rheumatoid arthritis has been demonstrated by immunofluorescent methods.

Rheumatoid factors may be detected by a variety of techniques, most involving agglutination reactions. These use a suspension of particles coated with IgG. For example, sheep red blood cells may be coated with rabbit anti-sheep-red-cell antibody (immune binding); or inert particles, such as tanned red cells or latex or bentonite particles, may be coated with heat-aggregated human IgG (nonimmune binding). Dilutions of the serum being tested are added to the suspension of particles. Agglutination on addition of a certain titer of serum (the titer differing in the different test systems) is indicative of the presence of rheumatoid factors in the serum being tested, and the test is read as positive. The result may be reported as the highest titer producing agglutination. Because of satisfactory clinical experience and technical convenience, the Fraction II Latex Fixation test of Singer and Plotz[20] has been adopted for general use. Other test systems may offer advantages in specific research situations.

As has been emphasized by many investigators, the detection of rheumatoid factors does not establish the presence of rheumatoid arthritis, nor does its absence exclude this diagnosis. However, since a large majority of patients with definite rheumatoid arthritis have rheumatoid factors, their detection has considerable diagnostic significance, and is included as one of the American Rheumatism Association's eleven criteria for rheumatoid arthritis.[21]

Rheumatoid factors may be present in other conditions. About one-quarter of patients with systemic lupus erythematosus (SLE), scleroderma, and polymyositis will have positive latex fixation tests. Some patients with juvenile rheumatoid arthritis have rheumatoid factors, but their incidence is much lower than in the adult form of the disease. Rheumatoid factors usually are absent from the sera of patients with ankylosing spondylitis or with arthritis associated with ulcerative colitis, and occur only rarely in patients with psoriasis and accompanying arthritis. They also are seen in some nonrheumatic disorders, such as chronic liver disease, and may appear transiently in certain viral infections, leprosy, and syphilis. Of particular interest is the high incidence of rheumatoid factors in patients with subacute bacterial endocarditis[22] and in kidney transplant recipients.[23] In these two situations a major disturbance of host defense mechanisms exists. Rheumatoid factors are rarely found in healthy persons, though an increased incidence with age has been reported.

In a patient with rheumatoid arthritis, a positive test for rheumatoid factors, if it is to occur, tends to develop fairly early in the course of the disease—within the first year or two. Therefore, except in this early stage, there is little correlation between the presence of rheumatoid factors and the duration of the disease. There is, however, a strong impression that a positive test for rheumatoid factors, particularly in high titer, has certain prognostic implications. It is associated with an increased probability of an unremitting course and more severe joint involvement, as manifested by x-ray changes.[8] Other reports suggest that nodules,[24] skin lesions, and systemic involvement are particularly likely to occur in patients with very high titers of rheumatoid factors. In an individual patient, the titer of rheumatoid factors may or may not vary with clinical exacerbation and remission.

The role of rheumatoid factors in the pathogenesis of rheumatoid arthritis is not clear. Acute arthritis has been induced in patients with seropositive rheumatoid arthritis by the intra-articular injection of autologous IgG globulin, while similar injections in patients with rheumatoid arthritis, but without rheumatoid factors, did not result in synovitis.[25] On the other hand, prolonged infusion of rheumatoid plasma in normal subjects has had no deleterious effect.[26] Moreover, definite of classical rheumatoid arthritis may occur in patients without rheumatoid factors in their serum and there is a high incidence of rheumatoid arthritis in patients with agammaglobulinemia.

F. Lupus Erythematosus (LE) Cell and Antinuclear Antibodies (ANA)

The lupus erythematosus cell, which was described by Hargraves in 1948, forms after blood or other body fluid has been incubated, unclotted, for two hours.[27] It forms when the lupus erythematosus factor (an antinuclear antibody) in the blood of the patient reacts with the nuclear material, and the homogeneous substance, which has the appearance of ground glass, is phagocytized by a polymorphonuclear leukocyte. The final appearance is a poly, with its nucleus compressed to the periphery by the large globular homogeneous mass. This same material may be seen free extracellularly prior to phagocytosis. The phenomenon occurs in many but not all patients with systemic lupus erythematosus, is relatively specific although it can occur in other connective tissue diseases, and has its counterpart in the tissue in the hematoxylin body. The serum factor has been identified as an antinuclear antibody (antibody to nucleoprotein) usually of the IgG class, but occasionally of the IgA or IgM class. This test is very useful, but in many laboratories has been supplanted by the antinuclear antibody tests.[28] Antinuclear factors (ANF) or antinuclear antibodies (ANA)[29,30] are antibodies directed against constituents of the cell nucleus. Those reactive with nucleoprotein are responsible for the lupus erythematosus cell phenomenon. These antibodies have been found in three immunoglobulin classes—IgG, IgA, and IgM—and are usually demonstrated by an immunofluorescent technique.

The antinuclear antibodies have been demonstrated by a variety of procedures, including:
- morphologic changes in cells (i.e., lupus erythematosus cell formation)
- coating of inert particles (latex or red blood cell) with the antigen and the observation of agglutination on exposure to the antibody
- identification of antigen-antibody by complement fixation or precipitin reactions
- immunofluorescent demonstration of the antibody, which is the most commonly used technique.

In the immunofluorescent demonstration of the antibody, tissue or cells used as substrate are first exposed to the serum being tested. When the serum is washed off, the specific antibody, if present, remains and is identified by fluorescein-tagged antibody, prepared in animals against human immunoglobulins. After further washing, the tissue is examined by fluorescent microscopy. If antinuclear factors are present, and fixed to the nuclei, they will have been labeled by the fluorescein-tagged antibody and the nuclei will appear as bright objects against a dark background. A number of patterns of nuclear fluorescence have been described (homogeneous, shaggy, speckled, and others) and clinical significance has been attributed to certain patterns, as described below.

Pattern	Significance
Homogeneous	Most common; antinucleoprotein antibody. Seen primarily in systemic lupus erythematosus, but occurs in other diseases as well.
Shaggy (peripheral or rim)	Represents antibody to DNA; more specific for systemic lupus erythematosus; often associated with disease activity, especially renal disease.
Speckled	Antibody to one of several soluble nuclear proteins; seen in systemic lupus erythematosus and in other diseases; associated by some with scleroderma.

Other patterns of uncertain significance have also been described.

Antinuclear antibodies are associated primarily with systemic lupus erythematosus, but occur in other rheumatic diseases as well and are found in the serum of 10 to 30 percent of patients with rheumatoid arthritis.[31] They are usually present in lower titers and demonstrate a homogeneous pattern. The antibody is likely to be in the IgM class. In systemic lupus erythematosus the titers are higher, a wider variety of patterns may be seen, some of which are almost specific for systemic lupus erythematosus, and the antibody is more commonly an IgG.

While these tests are useful clinically, detailed serologic studies, which are not always readily available, have further defined the antibodies to nuclear constituents of systemic lupus erythematosus. For example, antibodies occur to:
- native DNA (double-stranded) (NDNA)
- denatured DNA (single-stranded) (SDNA)
- Nucleoprotein
- Sm Antigen, carbohydrate protein antigen, and possibly others
- RNA-protein (ENA),

as well as antibodies to cytoplasmic constituents, RNA antibodies, etc. Immune complexes to a number of these constituents have also been described in the serum and related to disease activity.[32] It is now known that SDNA is seen in many diseases, although it occurs in highest titers in systemic lupus erythematosus. NDNA is seen in high concentration in other disease states but high-titered NDNA-antibodies seem to be unique to systemic lupus erythematosus, while SDNA antibodies are not.

During remission or during treatment with steroids and immunosuppressive agents, the titers of all the antinuclear constitutents may decrease significantly or disappear from the serum. The diagnosis of systemic lupus erythematosus does not depend solely upon this serologic factor. The history, physical, and other laboratory findings must be considered. The American Rheumatism Association established criteria for the classifications of systemic lupus erythematosus in 1971, and these factors should be considered collectively in comparing patients with systemic lupus erythematosus.[33]

G. Complement (C¹.)

The nine distinct serum proteins that interact sequentially and mediate aspects of antigen-antibody reactions have been termed the complement system.[34,35] Most laboratories can perform assays for only a limited number of these components (C3, C4) or determine the whole hemolytic complement activity (CH50). There are many technical problems, including those involved with sample handling, that must be considered when evaluating such laboratory data, but the system is of potential clinical value in rheumatic diseases.

In general, patients with rheumatoid arthritis will have normal or elevated serum complement (C[1]) levels while those with systemic lupus erythematosus, especially if the disease is active, will have decreased levels.[35] It has recently been suggested that the complement level may be decreased in rheumatoid patients with high titer rheumatoid factors, nodules, and vasculitis.[36] Serum complement levels in most other inflammatory conditions are generally increased, and complement may be likened in these instances clinically to the acute phase reactants.

Synovial fluid complement levels in rheumatoid-factor-positive fluids are generally decresed while seronegative rheumatoid arthritis fluids may be normal or increased. Synovial fluid complement in systemic lupus erythematosus generally is decreased. In most other acute inflammations of the synovium (i.e., gout, pseudogout, infection) the complement of synovial fluid may be decreased, normal, or increased.[34,35]

Depressed complement levels suggest its consumption in an immune reaction. While this is the case in many circumstances, it may also be decreased due to decreased synthesis or increased utilization. It is to be expected that as clinical correlations with specific clinical conditions are developed, and as the tests become more readily available and reproducible, complement determinations will assume a more significant role in the evaluation of the rheumatic diseases.

REFERENCES

1. Cohen, A. S.: Laboratory Diagnostic Procedures in the Rheumatic Diseases, *Boston, Little, Brown and Company, 1967, 2nd edition, 1974.*

2. Hollander, J. L. and McCarty, D. J., Jr., eds.: Arthritis and Allied Conditions, *8th edition, Philadelphia, Lea & Febiger, 1972.*

3. McCarty, D. J. and Hollander, J. L.: Identification of urate crystals in gouty synovial fluid, Ann. Intern. Med. 54:452, March 1961.

4. McCarty, D. J., Jr., Kohn, N. N., and Faires, J. S.: The significance of calcium phosphate crystals in the synovial fluid of arthritic patients: the "pseudogout syndrome," Ann. Intern. Med. 56:711, May 1962.

5. Skinner, M. and Cohen, A. S.: Calcium pyrophosphate dihydrate crystal deposition disease, Arch. Intern. Med. 123:626, June 1969.

6. Newcombe, D. S. and Cohen, A. S.: Chylous synovial effusion in rheumatoid arthritis: clinical and pathogenetic significance, Amer. J. Med. 38:156, January 1965.

7. Short, C. L., Bauer, W., and Reynolds, W. E.: Rheumatoid Arthritis, *Cambridge, Mass., Harvard University Press, 1957.*

8. Sharp, J. T., Calkins, E., Cohen, A.S., Schubart, A. F., and Calabro, J. J.: Observations on the clinical, chemical, and serological manifestations of rheumatoid arthritis, based on the course of 154 cases, Medicine 43:41, 1964.

9. Westergren, A.: The technique of the red cell sedimentation reaction, Amer. Rev. Tuberc. 14:*94, 1926.*

10. Fischel, E. E.: The erythrocyte sedimentation rate. In Laboratory Diagnostic Procedures in the Rheumatic Diseases, *ed. A. S. Cohen, 2nd edition, Boston, Little, Brown and Company, 1974.*

11. Fischel, E. E.: The C-reactive protein. In Laboratory Diagnostic Procedures in the Rheumatic Diseases, *ed. A. S. Cohen, 2nd edition, Boston, Little, Brown and Company, 1974.*

12. Sørensen, L. B.: The elimination of uric acid in man: studied by means of C¹⁴-labeled uric acid, Scand. J. Clin. Lab. Invest. 12 (Suppl. 54):*1, 1960.*

13. Wyngaarden, J. B. and Kelley, W. N.: Gout. In The Metabolic Basis of Inherited Disease, *ed. J. B. Stanbury, J. B. Wyngaarden, and D. S. Fredrickson, 3rd edition, New York, McGraw-Hill, 1972.*

14. Seegmiller, J. E.: Serum uric acid. In Laboratory Diagnostic Procedures in the Rheumatic Diseases, *ed. A. S. Cohen, 2nd edition, Boston, Little, Brown and Company, 1974.*

15. Wyngaarden, J. B.: Metabolic defects of primary hyperuricemia and gout, Amer. J. Med. 56:*651, 1974.*

16. Garrod, A. B.: Observations on certain pathologic conditions of the blood and urine in gout, rheumatism, and Bright's disease, Medico-Chir. Trans. 31:*83, 1848.*

17. Grayzel, A. I., Liddle, L., and Seegmiller, J. E.: Diagnostic significance of hyperuricemia in arthritis, New Eng. J. Med. 265:*763, October 19, 1961.*

18. Cathcart, E. S.: Rheumatoid factors: serologic techniques. In Laboratory Diagnostic Procedures in the Rheumatic Diseases, *ed. A. S. Cohen, 2nd edition, Boston, Little, Brown and Company, 1974.*

19. Christian, C. L.: Nature and significance of rheumatoid factors. In Laboratory Diagnostic Procedures in the Rheumatic Diseases, *ed. A. S. Cohen, 2nd edition, Boston, Little, Brown and Company, 1974.*

20. Singer, J. M. and Plotz, C. M.: The latex fixation test. I. Application to the serologic diagnosis of rheumatoid arthritis, Amer. J. Med. 21:*888, December 1956.*

21. Ropes, M. W., Bennett, G. A., Cobb, S., Jacox, R., and Jessar, R. A.: 1958 revision of diagnostic criteria for rheumatoid arthritis, Bull. Rheum. Dis. 9:*175, December 1958.*

22. Williams, R. C., Jr. and Kunkel, H. G.: Rheumatoid factor, complement, and conglutinin aberrations in patients with subacute bacterial endocarditis, J. Clin. Invest. 41:*666, 1962.*

23. Bravo, J. F., Herman, J. H., and Smyth, C. J.: Musculoskeletal disorders after renal homotransplantation: a clinical and laboratory analysis of 60 cases, Ann. Intern. Med. 66:*87, January 1967.*

24. Franklin, E. C., Kunkel, H. G., and Ward, J. R.: Clinical studies of seven patients with rheumatoid arthritis and uniquely large amounts of rheumatoid factor, Arthritis Rheum. 1:*400, 1958.*

25. Restifo, R. A., Lussier, A. J., Rawson, A. J., Rockey, J. H., and Hollander, J. L.: Studies on the pathogenesis of rheumatoid joint inflammation. III. The experimental production of arthritis by the intra-articular injection of purified 7S gamma globulin, Ann. Intern. Med. 62:*285, February 1965.*

26. Vaughan, J. H. and Harris, J.: Transfusion of rheumatoid plasma and cells, Arthritis Rheum. 2:*51, 1959.*

27. Hargraves, M. M.: Discovery of the LE cell and its morphology, Mayo Clin. Proc. 44:*579, September 1969.*

Cohen

28. *Beck, J. S.: Antinuclear antibodies: methods of detection and significance, Mayo Clin. Proc.* 44:*600, September 1969.*

29. *Friou, G. J.: Antinuclear antibodies: diagnostic significance and methods, Arthritis Rheum.* 10:*151, April 1967.*

30. *Friou, G. J.: The LE cell factor and antinuclear antibodies. In* Laboratory Diagnostic Procedures in the Rheumatic Diseases, *ed. A. S. Cohen, 2nd edition, Boston, Little, Brown and Company, 1974.*

31. *Condemi, J. J., Barnett, E. V., Atwater, E. C., Jacox, R. F., Mongan, E. S., and Vaughan, J. H.: The significance of antinuclear factors in rheumatoid arthritis, Arthritis Rheum.* 8:*1080, December 1965.*

32. *Agnello, V., Koffler, D., and Kunkel, H. G.: Immune complex systems in the nephritis of systemic lupus erythematosus, Kidney International* 3:*90, 1973.*

33. *Cohen, A. S., Reynolds, W. E., Franklin, E. C., Kulka, J. P., Ropes, M. W., Shulman, L. E., and Wallace, S. L.: Preliminary criteria for the classification of systemic lupus erythematosus, Bull. Rheum. Dis.* 21:*643, May 1971.*

34. *Austen, K. F. and Ruddy, S.: Serum and synovial fluid complement. In* Laboratory Diagnostic Procedures in the Rheumatic Diseases, *ed. A. S. Cohen, 2nd edition, Boston, Little, Brown and Company, 1974.*

35. *Schur, P. H. and Austen, K. F.: Complement in the rheumatic diseases, Bull. Rheum. Dis.* 22:*666, 1971-72.*

36. *Franco, A. E. and Schur, P. H.: Hypocomplementemia in rheumatoid arthritis, Arthritis Rheum.* 14:*231, March-April 1971.*

CHAPTER 4

The Roles of Patient and Physician in the Management of Arthritis

Richard H. Freyberg, M.D., M.A.C.P.
Emeritus Clinical Professor of Medicine and Chief
Division of Rheumatic Diseases
Cornell University Medical College
New York, New York

Emeritus Director
Department of Rheumatic Diseases
Hospital for Special Surgery
New York, New York

CHAPTER 4

The Roles of Patient and Physician in the Management of Arthritis

Richard H. Freyberg, M.D., M.A.C.P.

A. Introduction

Proper management of the patient with arthritis is governed by three considerations:
- the type of arthritis
- the severity of the symptoms
- the extent of the disease

Though these considerations apply to all forms of arthritis, they are most important for the chronic types and apply for general measures of treatment as well as special therapeutic procedures. In this discussion of general measures, emphasis will be placed on the chronic types of arthritis—rheumatoid arthritis, degenerative joint disease (osteoarthritis), and gout.

The most important consideration in the management and provision of care for the patient is determining a specific diagnosis. This depends upon thorough study of the patient initially and upon frequent follow-up examination (see Chapter 2). When the physician has identified the type of arthritis, he has built the foundation for planning effective management. It is almost equally important for the patient to know the nature of his illness and what it will mean to him physically, psychologically, economically, and socially. It is the responsibility of the managing physician to instruct the patient regarding these important aspects of his disease. Likewise, responsible members of the patient's family should understand the nature of the illness and how it may affect their way of life. If the patient is a child, the parents should be properly instructed.

B. Important Patient Information

In all chronic forms of arthritis, the patient must understand how best to live with his disease, realizing that he has a long-term illness that may continue for the rest of his life. The more he knows about his illness, the better he will adjust to and accept it, the better will be his cooperation in the management program, and the better will be the results. The patient needs guidance from his physician about adjustments in his manner of living that will make it easier for him to live with a painful and potentially disabling illness. This may require many sessions with the physician, who should be patient but candid in his explanations. At all times the physician should be as optimistic and encouraging as the patient's condition allows.

When told that he has arthritis, the patient usually thinks of the worst consequences. He recalls friends or relatives who became crippled or even totally disabled, and he fears this will be his plight. In general, depending on the nature of his condition, he should be told that there are many forms of arthritis, that many are not chronic and produce little or no crippling, that there are great differences in the nature and severity of each form of arthritis, and that the prognosis may not be as bad as he thinks.

1. Rheumatoid arthritis
The patient with rheumatoid arthritis needs to be told that this form of arthritis, if it progresses and cannot be suppressed, may cause joint damage and deformities. He should be told that crippling and disability sometimes occur, but that with proper treatment, begun in the early stages of the disease, such consequences often can be prevented or kept to a minimum. It is essential that he understand the importance of cooperating in a long-term treatment program, which will require frequent review and adjustment during the course of the chronic illness.

It should be emphasized to the patient with rheumatoid arthritis that the course of the disease is characterized by remission and relapses, and the pattern cannot be predicted at any given time. The patient is encouraged to learn that many people have mild disease that is completely arrested and remains in complete remission without producing significant deformities or crippling; that in many people the disease may be only moderately active and can be kept under control and thereby prevent serious disability; that while there is no cure, treatment can arrest the activity of the disease in most cases; that only a minority of patients have such severe cases that joint damage, crippling, and disability occur in spite of strict adherence to the treatment program; and that exacerbations are unpredictable, require special treatment, and are not necessarily a sign of serious long-term problems. When the patient understands this, it is easier for him to accept the need for frequent visits to his physician for evaluation of his progress and to determine if changes in his treatment program should be made.

As a group, patients with juvenile rheumatoid arthritis have a better prognosis than adults. In many children the disease becomes inactive around puberty. This and other aspects of the disease should be explained to the parents. With full knowledge, the parents and the patient will cooperate better with the physician in the treatment program, and this will minimize joint damage during the active period of the disease.

2. Osteoarthritis

The patient with osteoarthritis should be told that his condition is entirely different from rheumatoid arthritis, that it usually is confined to a few weight-bearing joints and widespread disease and deformity are not to be expected, and that the prognosis generally is much better than in rheumatoid arthritis. He should realize, however, that although systemic deterioration is not characteristic of the disease, irreversible damage to the joint cartilages and bone may occur, which will cause pain and disability in the affected joint. Progression of the degenerative process may cease at any stage, and many patients end up with only minor joint disability. Pain usually stops when progression of the degenerative pathology ceases. When the patient with osteoarthritis understands his disease, when he realizes that he need not fear widespread joint damage and disability, he is likely to feel relieved and to accept the problem of localized joint disability. The value of continued medical supervision in preventing unnecessary disability should be emphasized.

Osteoarthritis is the most common form of arthritis. Because of its degenerative nature, it usually affects the elderly; indeed, it appears to be an inherent part of aging. However, its appearance is not always an indication of generalized aging. Many people think of osteoarthritis as a sign of arterial or vital organ deterioration and impending death. Patients should be assured that many people with their condition have little or no change in vital organ function and live long, happy lives, with only the nuisance of one or two involved joints causing limited difficulty in locomotion. Middle-aged patients whose osteoarthritis results from injury or infection should be assured that they are healthy in all other respects.

3. Ankylosing spondylitis

Ankylosing spondylitis primarily affects young men. Patients should be informed that they will probably have pain in the back and hips or shoulders for several years, and that the disease tends to spread slowly up the spine to cause pain and stiffness. They should understand that the disease can cease to be active at any time, usually 10 to 15 years after onset, and this results in rigidity of the spine, but little or no pain. The patient should be informed that the spine will remain rigid in the position in which it becomes ankylosed so that he will cooperate in a program to prevent persistent spinal deformity.

4. Gout

Gout is characterized by attacks of painful joint inflammation, usually of short duration. The attacks generally last 5 to 10 days and are followed by long intervals of good health. Only if the disease goes untreated for many years does the joint disorder become chronic and disabling. The arthritis of gout results from a metabolic disorder of purine metabolism due either to a genetic, inherited metabolic disorder (primary gout) or to an acquired disorder induced by drugs taken for other illnesses. Patients with gout should be assured that they do not have rheumatoid arthritis, osteoarthritis, or other progressive arthritic disease and that with proper treatment their metabolic disorder usually can be controlled to prevent attacks and chronic joint damage. The patient should understand that it is essential to continue treatment for the rest of his life (if primary gout) or for as long as he is exposed to the precipitating cause (if acquired gout). He should be instructed regarding the factors that may precipitate attacks so that they can be avoided.

5. Other rheumatic diseases

Some patients have symptoms of joint disease due to nonarticular rheumatic disturbances—bursitis, tendinitis, tenosynovitis, fibrositis, etc. These disorders should be recognized and differentiated from arthritis, and patients should be told that they do not have progressive arthritis, that they need not fear deformities or disability resulting from joint damage, and that the prognosis is good. It should be emphasized that they have a minor form of rheumatism that usually can be relieved with conservative treatment.

Trauma and many microbial infections may cause arthritis. In such cases, the patient should be informed about the nature of his joint disease and should be told that, with proper treatment, he does not have a form of arthritis that will continue to progress and cause disability or crippling.

It is clear that the managing physician has primary responsibility of properly diagnosing the arthritic or rheumatic condition and informing the patient about his disease and what it means to him and his family. The patient should be candidly informed about treatment procedures, their purpose, their limitations, and what he can look forward to in the future. This way, the patient is more likely to cooperate fully with his physician, carrying out a well-planned management program that often produces gratifying, therapeutic benefit.

To help the physician educate his arthritic patients, the Arthritis Foundation has prepared separate booklets for patients with rheumatoid arthritis, osteoarthritis, gout, and arthritis in general.[1] These booklets can be obtained from local chapters of the foundation.

C. The Management Program

Successful treatment of any form of arthritis depends upon formulating a proper program of management and carrying it out throughout the clinically active period of the disease, whether acute or chronic. No single form of treatment is adequate for all patients with any type of arthritis. Rather, therapy requires blending many treatment procedures into a program adapted to the specific needs of each patient. The program may require frequent changes to accommodate changes in the patient's condition at different stages of his disease. It must be planned properly to meet specific objectives and usually embodies several different modalities of treatment. Although the program differs for each type of arthritis and for each patient, some common objectives can be noted that can be adapted to the needs of the individual patient. These objectives include:
  □ relief of pain
  □ maintenance of maximal joint function
  □ suppression of active arthritis
  □ prevention of deformities
  □ maintenance of proper diet and nutrition
  □ treatment of concurrent illness and complications
  □ correction of deformities and rehabilitation

Note that the following discussion covers general treatment measures for arthritic patients. Some patients require special measures that are discussed in other chapters.

1. Relief of pain
The chief complaint of patients with any form of arthritis is pain—pain with movement of joints in performing the routine activities of daily living and that can lead to restricted movement and stiffness. Since this symptom is the patient's primary concern, it should receive priority in planning the general measures of treatment.

The pain, aching, and stiffness of arthritis can be relieved by three different modalities of treatment: analgesic medication, rest from excessive and aggravating physical activity, and physical therapy.

a. Aspirin

The basic, most reliable, and best tolerated medication for relief of arthritis pain is aspirin, but it must be used properly to obtain the best possible results. The therapeutic value is comparable for all brands of aspirin given in equal dosage. Some patients may prefer specific brands because of fewer side effects or greater speed of action—attributes imparted by constituents of the tablet other than the active ingredients.

The first rule of aspirin dosage is to give as much as is needed to accomplish maximal analgesia or as much as can be tolerated. Aspirin is more effective and better tolerated when given in divided doses at prescribed intervals. Effectiveness is diminished when taken at the patient's discretion to control intense pain. For the average-size adult (125 to 175 pounds) with moderately severe arthritis, 650 mg (10 grains: 2 tablets) four times daily, a total of 2.6 g in 24 hours, is the most frequently satisfactory dosage schedule. For larger adults and for those with more severe pain, larger doses may be needed, sometimes reaching 1 g four or five times a day. The conventional dosage schedule is the first dose at breakfast, the second at lunch, the third at supper, and the fourth at bedtime. If five doses are needed, the additional dose usually is taken during the night when the patient awakens with pain.

The side effects that most frequently require dosage limitation are tinnitus followed by loss of hearing acuity, gastrointestinal irritation causing burning epigastric discomfort, a feeling of gastric distention, sour eructations, nausea, and vomiting. These symptoms are due largely, if not entirely, to the acidity of aspirin. A common clinical indication of excess dosage is tinnitus. When this symptom occurs, the medication should be discontinued until the tinnitus subsides and should then be resumed in smaller doses, just below the tinnitus-provoking level.

Gastrointestinal symptoms occur much more often and more severely if aspirin is taken when the stomach is empty. Therefore, the drug should be taken with meals or an antacid. Food is a good buffer for the gastrointestinal irritation of aspirin, but if the patient is overweight or needs additional buffering, any of the antacid medicines commonly prescribed for reduction of gastric acidity—the aluminum hydroxide gels—should be prescribed in tablet or liquid form with each dose of aspirin. Some patients tolerate buffered aspirin better than plain aspirin. While the buffering may sometimes lessen the side effects of aspirin, it does not enhance the analgesic effect.

Prolonged gastrointestinal irritation from aspirin may cause mucosal ulceration and bleeding (usually mild). Peptic ulcer has occurred in a small percentage of patients who have taken large amounts of aspirin over prolonged periods of time.

b. Special considerations in the use of aspirin

Deviation from the conventional aspirin dosage schedule may be required, depending on the type of arthritis being treated, the age of the patient, the severity of the disease, the severity of the pain, and the presence of a complicating illness.

Rheumatoid arthritis

In patients with mild rheumatoid arthritis involving few joints and producing little inflammation, lower dosages of aspirin are often adequate. In these patients, 650 mg two or three times daily may suffice. Larger dosages should not be used unless they are needed. In severe disease with widespread involvement and much joint inflammation, as much as 5 or 6 g daily may be required. With these larger doses, great care must be taken to avoid salicylism. When very large doses are used, blood salicylate levels should be determined frequently to keep the blood level below the toxic level (usually less than 30 mg percent).

To provide greater relief of morning stiffness, which may be severe and prolonged in patients with severe rheumatoid arthritis, it is frequently helpful to administer 650 mg of aspirin an hour or two prior to arising from bed in the morning. Aching and pain during the long period in bed at night may be more effectively relieved by taking a large dose of slowly absorbed aspirin, which sustains the anti-inflammatory effect for six to eight hours.

In patients who have an active peptic ulcer or severe gastric irritation, it is desirable to use enteric-coated aspirin, which is released from the tablet and absorbed after it passes from the stomach into the intestine.

If aspirin in any form cannot be tolerated, substitute medication should be tried. As a rule, the substitutes that are tolerated are less analgesic, but they may provide sufficient relief and avoid the need for narcotics and other more potent agents. Acetaminophen is often used as a substitute for aspirin. In some patients, 650 mg (two tablets) four or five times daily provides satisfactory relief and is well tolerated.

Rheumatoid patients with severe pain may require other analgesic medication to supplement the effects of aspirin. Propoxyphene hydrochloride in a dosage of 65 mg two to four times daily may substitute for aspirin, or it can be combined with aspirin, phenacetin, and caffeine, which together often produce greater analgesia than obtained from either medication alone.

Control of severe rheumatic pain seldom requires narcotic drugs. Narcotics should not be used for prolonged periods because of the danger of habituation and addiction. For periods of a few days, narcotics may be justified to alleviate severe pain. Meperidine is the preferred narcotic; usually 50 mg one to three times daily will suffice. Codeine, 32 mg once or twice during the night, may relieve severe pain and allow sleep.

Other medications are used primarily for their anti-inflammatory effect, but they also have analgesic value. These agents will be discussed in Chapter 6.

Juvenile rheumatoid arthritis

The symptoms of juvenile rheumatoid arthritis may at times be very severe, characterized by fever and great pain in inflamed joints. At such times, large amounts of aspirin may be needed, but the dosage should always be determined in relationship to the size of the child. For maintenance, 90 to 130 mg per kg of body weight per day is often required. Most children can tolerate aspirin in moderately large doses for prolonged periods. When high doses are given, care must be exercised to prevent toxicity. In such cases, it is desirable to base the dosage on the blood salicylate level. As improvement occurs, the dosage should be lowered gradually. This reduced dosage may be required for many months or years. For infants and small children, tablets containing small amounts of aspirin are available ("children's aspirin"). Solutions that have a pleasant taste (e.g., choline salicylate) are also available.

Rheumatic fever

The pain of arthritis from active rheumatic fever is often very severe, but fortunately it generally responds remarkably well to full-dose aspirin. Aspirin usually is started at 100 mg per kg of body weight, and increased, if tolerated, up to 3 g daily in children and up to 6 g daily in adults. The plasma salicylate level should be kept at 25 to 30 mg per 100 ml. Treatment must be continued for many weeks after clinical signs of disease activity abate. The dosage should be decreased slowly. Disease activity may recur if the drug is discontinued too early.

Other diffuse connective tissue diseases

The arthritis of systemic lupus erythematosus is often very similar to rheumatoid arthritis, and it is difficult to differentiate between the two. However, systemic lupus erythematosus usually includes visceral and other nonarticular disease and thus requires treatment with drugs more potent than aspirin (see Chapter 6). In mild cases, aspirin used in a manner similar to that advised for rheumatoid arthritis is a satisfactory analgesic for the arthritic pain. Since patients with systemic lupus erythematosus tolerate all drugs poorly, especially careful supervision is required at all times. The illness is frequently very complicated and the managing physician would do well to consult with a rheumatologist or refer the patient to a clinical center.

The same advice is appropriate for patients with other diffuse connective tissue disorders, such as progressive systemic sclerosis (scleroderma), polymyositis (dermatomyositis), and polyarteritis.

The rheumatic pain of gouty arthritis responds better to drugs other than aspirin (see Chapter 6).

Ankylosing spondylitis often responds well to conventional dosages of aspirin, but many patients require other drugs, such as phenylbutazone or indomethacin (see Chapter 6).

Osteoarthritis
Osteoarthritis should be treated for analgesic relief in a manner similar to that described for rheumatoid arthritis. Narcotic drugs should be restricted to short-term use and should be given only for severe pain. Some patients with osteoarthritis of the hip (malum coxae senilis) respond better to small doses of indomethacin, such as 25 mg two or three times daily with food, than to other medications (see Chapter 6).

Patients with traumatic arthritis or acute infectious arthritis may need narcotics as a supplement to aspirin for short-term relief. Aspirin usually is sufficient for mild or moderate cases.

Local topical analgesics—the counter-irritants such as liniment containing methyl salicylate or similar rubefacients—may provide mild short-term relief of arthritic pain. However, these preparations usually are not adequate for maximal relief of pain and should be used as supplemental therapy only.

2. Maintenance of maximal joint function
a. Rest and restriction of activity
Rest meets several objectives of the management program. It contributes to relief of pain, preservation of joint movement, and maintenance of good general health. Though it is difficult to say how much rest a specific patient should have, general principles can be stated. For chronic arthritis, the more widespread and severe the illness, the greater the amount of rest required.

Acute arthritis often requires almost complete rest of the involved joints. Systemic illness, especially with fever, requires complete bed rest usually during the febrile period. Excessive rest can do harm by contributing to muscle atrophy and joint stiffness; insufficient rest or excessive activity can result in prolongation of illness and greater joint damage. For these reasons, rest and activity must always be considered together and kept in proper balance.

Different types of rest must be considered: complete body rest (systemic rest or bed rest), articular rest (local rest of the affected joints), and emotional rest. Systemic rest restricts total body movement of weight-bearing activity (walking, running, stair climbing, standing), while local rest restricts only the activity of affected joints.

The patient with arthritis tends to self-prescribe rest as part of his treatment. From experience he quickly learns that movement of an arthritic joint initiates or aggravates the arthralgia, and restricting movement of the affected joints provides relief. Consequently, he needs guidance to establish the right kind of rest and the proper balance between rest and activity. The rest-activity program differs with the type and localization of the arthritis.

In rheumatoid arthritis, patients with very active, widespread joint inflammation and manifestations of severe systemic disease—especially with fever, visceral involvement, or vasculitis—should have complete bed rest until the fever subsides and the visceral disease is controlled. This usually requires only a few days or weeks. Then graded increases in activity are appropriate, but activity should be kept below the level that causes fatigue or severe pain. While the patient is confined to bed, isometric or assisted exercises help to minimize the muscle atrophy and weakness that inevitably result from inactivity (see Chapter 5).

When control of rheumatoid arthritis was much less effective than it is today, many rheumatologists advised all patients with widespread arthritic involvement to have many months of complete or nearly complete bed rest. This now is considered not only unnecessary but inadvisable. A recent and well-controlled study[2] failed to show any value from bed rest of 22 to 24 hours a day compared to *ad lib* activity for patients with active rheumatoid arthritis.

For all but the febrile, severely ill patient, some activity through the daytime is to be encouraged. The amount of activity and rest depends largely upon the severity and extent of the disease and whether joints of locomotion are affected. Patients with many joints in all extremities involved need abundant daytime rest in bed or in a chair, but they should have one or two short periods of ambulatory activity daily, consisting of therapeutic exercises designed to put all affected joints through full or maximal range of motion (see Chapter 5). For the patient with only moderately active disease, two periods of systemic rest for one or two hours should be sufficient. The fortunate person with only a few small joints inflamed and little or no systemic illness needs no daytime systemic rest, but should have as much restriction of activity involving movement of the affected joints as is practical. During periods of exacerbation, more systemic rest is needed.

The location of joint involvement is an important factor in determining the amount of systemic and local rest to prescribe. It is generally agreed that weight-bearing activity tends to aggravate and prolong inflammation in weight-bearing joints. For this reason, it is advisable to minimize weight-bearing activity when hips, knees, ankles, feet, or low back are inflamed. A good rule for such patients is to sit instead of stand, ride instead of walk, and use the elevator instead of stairs. This way, the weight-bearing joints will get as much local rest as possible, and the patient will usually get as much systemic rest as needed. When only upper extremity joints are inflamed, non-weight-bearing rest is of little or no value, but it is important to have as much local rest of the affected joints as possible.

As a general rule, any painful joint, especially one that is inflamed, needs rest from movement. A variety of supports are available for this purpose, such as splints for small joints of the fingers, volar splints for the wrists, and light plaster molds (night rest splints) for the knees and ankles. Elastic ("Ace") bandages and tubular elastic supports are helpful for elbows, knees, and ankles. Metatarsal pads and bars on shoes transfer weight from toe joints to metatarsal shafts and provide articular rest for the toe joints. Slings are helpful to rest shoulder and elbow joints. These treatment devices are best provided by orthopedic surgeons, physical medicine experts, and occupational therapists, who should be consulted about local joint rest whenever possible (see Chapters 5 and 8).

Emotional rest is relief from stressful situations of business and household worries and is an asset to patients with prolonged, severe rheumatoid arthritis. If possible, the rheumatoid patient should be relieved of aggravating responsibilities and have assistance for stressful physical activities.

The arthritis of rheumatic fever requires systemic rest throughout the active disease. Local rest for larger joints, such as the use of sandbags, adds to the patient's comfort.

Osteoarthritis usually does not require systemic rest because it is not a systemic disease. Local rest, however, is of great importance and is very beneficial. Since osteoarthritis chiefly affects weight-bearing joints, avoiding weight-bearing activity and activity requiring movement of the affected joints helps lessen pain. When hips, knees, or feet are affected, a cane, elbow-length crutches, or axillary crutches provide local rest by transferring weight to the upper extremities. Sturdy supports are helpful for the osteoarthritic knee.

The spine is frequently involved in degenerative joint disease. Movement that causes or aggravates pain can be reduced by using local supports. For the cervical spine, felt or plastic collars are very helpful; for the lower back, rest on a firm bed, and the use of a flexible, steel-reinforced surgical corset support or rigid steel back brace when the patient is ambulatory may provide much relief.

In ankylosing spondylitis, it is very important to provide support to the back by using a firm bed with a shallow pillow or no pillow to keep the spine straight and thereby reduce the development of flexion deformity of the spine. Rigid braces, once popular for this type of spinal disorder, are now considered of little value.

Systemic therapeutic exercises should be done once or twice a day to maintain maximal movement of the spine. Such exercises should include guarded movements of the head and neck if the cervical spine is affected, and shoulder and hip exercises and gentle calisthenic exercises for the dorsal and lumbar spine. If the thoracic region is affected, deep-breathing exercises are needed to maintain maximal chest expansion.

When spinal, shoulder, or lower extremity joints are involved in any type of arthritis, therapeutic exercises are done much more effectively under warm water in a pool or Hubbard tank, where the warmth is a source of relief and the force of gravity is reduced by the buoyancy of the water. When possible, patients should be referred to a hospital or physical therapy unit having the proper equipment and staff to provide this type of treatment.

Acute gouty arthritis and acute gout caused by infection or trauma require complete rest of the affected articulations as long as the joint disease is active. Range of motion exercises are not required because of the short duration of active arthritis, but systemic and articular rest are very beneficial to relieve pain and hasten recovery.

The prudent use of sedatives and tranquilizers may substantially help the arthritic patient get the rest he needs. Chloral hydrate, phenobarbital, and sodium secobarbital are helpful for insomnia, but care should be taken to prevent dependency and habituation in patients with chronic illness. Small doses of phenobarbital, diazepam, or meprobamate may provide relief from tensions and apprehension during the daytime.

b. Heat as an analgesic
The application of heat from any source usually contributes substantially to relief of pain in practically all forms of arthritis. To obtain the greatest benefit, the patient should use heat two or three times a day throughout the duration of his illness. For chronic forms of arthritis this requires provision of a heat source in the patient's home.

The patient and responsible members of his family should be instructed in the modalities available and in the manner of their use.

Simple devices are usually as helpful as the elaborate and expensive ones. Warm baths for the entire body or for small areas, such as hand soaks, foot soaks, paraffin dips, compresses, and poultices, are effective and inexpensive sources of heat. Infrared lamps and "bakers" can be used in the home.

In more severe arthritis, a therapeutic pool or Hubbard tank with water heated to 92-94 degrees is of great value in providing simultaneous heat, exercise, and rest from gravity. In considering these forms of therapy, it should be kept in mind that specialty help can be obtained from physical medicine facilities of an arthritis treatment center or a large general hospital. Consultation with specialists is encouraged for all but the mild forms of arthritis (see Chapter 5).

3. Suppression of active arthritis

This extremely important objective should receive high priority in planning the management program for all forms of joint inflammation. Mild rheumatoid arthritis may be kept sufficiently suppressed by a good program of general management that provides proper analgesia, rest, and physical therapy. Progression of degenerative joint disease is lessened by avoiding stressful physical activity that requires prolonged weight bearing. However, for most types of inflammatory arthritis, suppression of disease activity usually cannot be accomplished by general treatment measures alone, and requires skillful use of special forms of treatment (see Chapters 6, 7, and 8).

4. Prevention of deformities

The physical therapeutic program described briefly earlier in this chapter and in more detail in Chapter 5 will do much to prevent deformities. A few important measures to meet this objective should be emphasized. Whenever joint disease prevents full range of movement at any articulation, and whenever prolonged systemic rest is required, flexion deformities may result. These deformities cannot always be prevented, but much can be done to minimize them.

A basic principle in the use of supports to provide rest of an inflamed joint is to keep the joint in a position that will allow most efficient function. This is done in case permanent restriction of movement or ankylosis occurs.

The following don'ts are an important part of the general management program:
- □ Don't rest for long periods with knees flexed, as required when sitting in a chair.

□ Don't put pillows under the knees when resting in bed. Keep the legs in a position of extension at the knees.

□ Don't keep arthritic hands resting with the radial (thumb) side dependent for long periods; rather, keep the ulnar side dependent to lessen tendency toward ulnar deviation of the fingers.

□ Don't favor flexion deformities at the hips by prolonged sitting in a chair or resting on a soft bed. The bed should be firm; a bed board may be needed.

□ Don't use a thick head pillow if upper dorsal and cervical spinal arthritis exists. Minimize flexion deformity of the upper spine by keeping the spine in as normal a position as possible when in bed. Since people spend about one third of their lives in bed, a proper position of rest is extremely important.

□ Don't neglect therapeutic range of motion exercises. They should be part of the daily routine.

□ Don't immobilize an inflamed joint in a plaster cast for prolonged periods.

Attention to these simple guidelines may significantly lessen deformities. Consultation with an orthopedic surgeon or physical medicine expert should be sought whenever complicated problems exist.

5. Maintenance of proper diet and nutrition

Patients with chronic arthritis frequently ask, "What should I eat?" "Should my diet include an abundance of certain foods; should any foods be restricted or excluded?" In general, the answer to these questions is that there is no "arthritis diet." Except for gout, exclusion of certain foods has no therapeutic value. The diet should contain the daily requirement of all food factors in amounts needed to provide good nutrition, and the caloric intake should be adjusted to bring the body weight to, or slightly below, the ideal healthy weight and keep it at that level. A well-balanced diet, providing the normal requirements of protein, carbohydrate, fat, minerals, and vitamins, will accomplish this goal. Many dietary fads have been recommended, some containing huge amounts of vitamins and minerals, others sharply eliminating carbohydrates, and still others providing an abundance of protein or fat. There has never been any scientific evidence to support claims of therapeutic value for these diets.

People with severe rheumatoid arthritis frequently lose weight and become undernourished. Such patients should have a high-caloric diet containing abundant protein, carbohydrate, and enough fat to bring the weight to normal and maintain it. This will improve the patient's systemic health and enable him to cope better with a prolonged, painful illness.

Frequent meals and appealing mixtures of nutritious foods, such as egg nogs, will aid in correcting undernutrition.

Some patients with rheumatoid arthritis and many with osteoarthritis are overweight. Excess weight produces extra stress in locomotion and increases the pain in arthritic weight-bearing joints. Body weight should be reduced through a low-calorie diet that is adequate in protein and all other essential food elements. When the weight has been brought to normal or slightly below normal, the caloric intake should be adjusted for maintenance.

A diet that includes fresh vegetables and fruits and adequate amounts of high quality protein foods will provide adequate vitamins and minerals to meet the nutritional requirements of optimal health. To assure adequate vitamin nutrition, a multi-vitamin complex can be taken as a supplement to the diet. Large supplements of any vitamin have not been proved to be of therapeutic value.

Of course, children with rheumatoid arthritis need a diet adequate in protein, calcium, and other foods essential for healthy growth. Severe disease often is accompanied by anorexia and general disinterest in food. The diet should be made as attractive and appealing as possible and should be presented in small portions, five or six times daily.

Gout is the only type of arthritis in which special dietary measures have therapeutic value. A large intake of purine foods may provoke an attack of gouty arthritis and will provide a larger source for uric acid production. However, with the proper use of a dependable uricosuric agent (probenecid) and an inhibitor of uric acid production from xanthine (allopurinol), it is not necessary to drastically limit the uric acid precursors, except in very severe gout. With these drugs, most patients need eliminate only the very cellular foods—chiefly liver, kidney, sweetbreads, and the like—and avoid large excesses of other protein foods.

Carbonated drinks, champagne, sparkling wines, and beer provoke acute attacks in some, but not all, gouty patients. If so, they should be avoided, along with any foods that appear to precipitate an acute attack in a specific patient. The best dietary principle for the gouty patient is to keep the type of food simple, eliminate glandular foods rich in purine, have meals at regular intervals, and avoid excesses of food and alcoholic beverages. Many patients with gout are overweight. The rules of diet to control weight discussed earlier apply to these patients.

Freyberg

6. Treatment of concurrent illnesses and complications

If good general health is maintained, the patient's natural resistance to chronic disabling arthritis will be greater and he will be better prepared to cope with painful rheumatic disease. All complicating diseases, infections, and other illnesses should be eliminated or controlled. Diseases unrelated to the arthritis should be treated in the manner appropriate for nonarthritic patients. During the years of illness with any chronic form of arthritis, disorders of viscera, endocrinopathies, infections, neoplastic disease, and other illness can be expected to occur; they should be recognized and properly treated.

Some medicines used to treat arthritis may cause troublesome side effects—dermatitis, stomatitis, gastrointestinal disorders, diarrhea, gastrointestinal bleeding, anemia, granulopenia, nervous system disorders, water retention, diuresis, etc. These complications should be recognized promptly. The offending medication should be identified and discontinued and appropriate remedies should be prescribed.

One of the most common complicating disorders is anemia. Unrelated primary anemia may be encountered as in any nonarthritic person. In rheumatoid arthritis anemia is characteristic of the systemic disease. Cause of this anemia is poorly understood and the condition is difficult to treat effectively. However, the most common form of anemia occurring in arthritic patients is iron deficiency anemia resulting from gastrointestinal bleeding. Even if bleeding cannot be identified, it must be suspected. Iron deficiency should be considered a cause or contributing factor to the anemic state and treatment with iron salts should be prescribed. Ferrous sulfate, 300 mg two or three times daily, or ferrous gluconate in comparable doses is the standard treatment.

7. Correction of deformities and rehabilitation

Because of neglect, inadequate treatment, or failure to respond even to excellent treatment, deformities and disability may result from extensive destructive changes to the joints and surrounding connective tissues. Much can be done to correct disabling deformities and to rehabilitate the crippled, even the invalid, arthritic patient. This requires the combined skills of specialists, especially the orthopedic surgeon. Management for these unfortunate arthritics extends beyond the scope of general treatment measures. Consultation with appropriate specialists and provision for care in an arthritis treatment center should be arranged so that the team effort of physician, surgeon, physical medicine expert, and other allied health professionals will be available to provide the comprehensive treatment program needed. (See also Chapters 5 and 8.)

80

REFERENCES

1. The following booklets are published by the Arthritis Foundation, 1212 Avenue of the Americas, New York, and are available from local chapters:

Arthritis—The Basic Facts

Rheumatoid Arthritis—A Handbook for Patients

Osteoarthritis—A Handbook for Patients

Gout—A Handbook for Patients

2. Mills, J. A. et al.: Value of bed rest in patients with rheumatoid arthritis, New Eng. J. Med. 284:453, March 4, 1971.

GENERAL REFERENCES

Hollander, J. L. and McCarty, D. J., Jr., eds.: Arthritis and Allied Conditions, *8th edition, Philadelphia, Lea & Febiger, 1972.*

Rodnan, G. P., McEwen, C., and Wallace, S. L.: Primer on the rheumatic diseases, JAMA 224 (Supplement), April 30, 1973.

Ehrlich, G. E.: Total Management of the Arthritic Patient, *Philadelphia, J. B. Lippincott, 1973.*

Freyberg, R. H.: Rheumatoid arthritis: the natural history, diagnosis, prognosis and management, Med. Times 95:724, July 1967.

CHAPTER 5

Guidelines for the
Physical Management and
Rehabilitation of the
Arthritic Patient

Robert L. Swezey, M.D., F.A.C.P.
Professor of Medicine and Rehabilitation Medicine
University of Southern California School of Medicine
Los Angeles, California

CHAPTER 5

Guidelines for the
Physical Management and
Rehabilitation of the
Arthritic Patient

Robert L. Swezey, M.D., F.A.C.P.

A. Introduction

Physical measures and surgical therapy may be essential to relieve pain and restore optimal function in the arthritis sufferer. A few basic principles govern the physical management and rehabilitation therapy plan.

▫ Painful articular structures are relieved by rest.
   Corollary:
      The more painful the condition the more total rest required.
▫ Both heat and cold can relieve pain.
   Corollaries:
      In acutely painful and especially in traumatic conditions, cold applications are more successful in relieving pain.
      In subacute and chronically painful conditions, superficial heating modalities (hot tub, warm moist compresses, paraffin dips) are more effective for pain relief.
      In selected deep, chronic, painful processes, deep heat (diathermy) may be of additional value as a pain-relieving agent.
▫ Exercise for the arthritic should restore mobility and strength without aggravating the arthritic process.
   Corollary:
      Exercises should be designed to cause the least possible pain and be repeated only as frequently as is essential to achieve their goal.

Severe trauma

Septic arthritis or osteomyelitis

Neurological deficit

Multiple progressive, acute or chronic, articular involvement

Unrelenting or increasing pain not controlled by current regimen

Increasing clinical or radiological evidence of joint destruction or deformity

Decreasing functional capability

Concurrent or complicating systemic or psychological disorders

TABLE 1
Guidelines for Consultation
or Referral to Rheumatic Disease Center

☐ The goals of therapy must be clear and must be reassessed constantly. Corollary:

New goals require new therapy. In a patient with a subsiding acute lumbar disc who is on a bed rest regimen, for example, the goals may change from total rest for pain relief to initiation of increasing activity and gentle spinal stretching exercises in order to begin restoring normal function.

Following these principles, one can implement a simple, effective therapeutic plan for most common arthritic disorders. Where complications are present or the response to therapy is unsatisfactory, consultation or arrangements for more comprehensive care should be made. The following cases will illustrate a balanced approach to physical treatment in a variety of common arthritic problems. In each case it is assumed that appropriate medications, including local steroid injections where indicated, are employed in conjunction with the physical and related rehabilitation therapy measures. Supplementary references for additional patient care resources are listed after each case discussion. Tables 1 and 2 provide an overview for quick reference.

PHYSICAL MANAGEMENT	STAGE OF DISEASE		
	Acute	Subacute	Chronic
Pain Relief	Cold compresses ± superficial heat	Superficial heat ± cold compresses	Superficial heat ± diathermy
Joint Rest	Immobilization up to 3 weeks maximum	Gradual mobilization	Stretch to restore maximum range
Splint, Brace, Corset	Yes	While joint is stressed	p.r.n. pain relief and stability
Joint Protection Measures	Rest and splint	Avoid trauma and strain. Employ assistive devices to minimize strain	Modify daily activities, and teach joint protection techniques
Traction	Occasionally for knee, neck, and low back	Usually for neck	Often for neck
Stretching Exercise	Gentle passive or active assisted, 1-3 repetitions, b.i.d.	Active assisted, 3-5 repetitions b.i.d., t.i.d.	5-10 repetitions for maximum stretch or prolonged static stretch
Strengthening Exercise	No	6-second isometric in position of maximum comfort, b.i.d.	Add repetitive and resistive exercises for endurance

TABLE 2

General Guidelines for Use of Physical Measures in Arthritis

87

B. Clinical Problems

1. Problem: Painful Neck
a. Acute cervical strain

A 19-year-old female is seen complaining of diffuse neck pain of 24 hours' duration radiating to the right shoulder. The onset immediately followed a wrenching of the neck in a poorly executed dive. Examination reveals an acutely painful, almost immobile, neck. X-rays reveal only straightening of the cervical lordotic curve. There are no neurological deficits.

Physical Treatment Plan

The following procedures are recommended: ice compresses for pain relief 20 minutes out of each hour; a plastic or felt cervical collar, to be worn both day and night, for protection against exacerbation of painful cervical motion; a small, firm bed pillow for use in rest and sleep.

Comment

In this acute and uncomplicated process, the primary goal is pain relief. As improvement occurs, pain will be relieved better by warm compresses. Range of motion exercises for the cervical spine will then be implemented to restore full mobility.

b. Subacute cervical strain

Three years later the same patient is seen complaining of an exacerbation of what has been a mild, intermittent, recurrent, painful neck problem. Examination reveals mild restriction of cervical rotation to the right and pain on full flexion of the neck. X-rays are within normal limits. There are no neurological deficits.

Physical Treatment Plan

Hot compresses for pain relief are prescribed and the patient is referred to a physical therapist for cervical traction. She is advised to resume wearing the collar if symptoms warrant. Exercises to restore cervical mobility are instituted when pain abates.

Comment

The patient now has a subacute exacerbation of a mildly painful cervical dysfunction. Cervical traction over a period of two to four weeks will usually benefit this problem. Hot compresses prior to the use of traction facilitate muscle relaxation. Depending on the degree of pain, the use of a cervical collar at this stage may be of value. Occasional patients with more persistent chronic pain are benefited by the addition of diathermy.

c. Cervical disc with radiculopathy

Seven years later the patient returns with a history of periodic mild neck discomfort. This pain was promptly relieved by resuming traction at home.

Neck pain on occasion has been severe enough to require wearing a cervical collar for a few days. Two weeks previously she stopped her car abruptly to avoid hitting a pedestrian. Since then she has had persistent pain in the lower cervical region, posteriorly radiating into the right shoulder with some numbness on the dorsal aspect of the right arm. Examination reveals a slight impairment of pain sensation over the dorsum of the right arm and weakness of the deltoid. X-rays show evidence of discogenic disease at C-5, C-6.

Physical Treatment Plan

Use of a cervical collar is resumed and, because of clear-cut neurological deficit, an orthopedic or neurosurgical consultation is requested.

References
Efficacy of heat and cold.[1-6]
Cervical traction.[7-11]

2. Problem: Acute and Chronic Low Back Pain
a. Acute lumbosacral strain

A 35-year-old housewife developed severe pain in the low back radiating into the left buttock while bending forward and attempting to lift a heavy shopping bag. Examination showed the patient to be in acute distress, with pain precipitated by any motion of her back. The right paralumbar muscles were in tense "spasm." Neurological examination was normal and x-rays revealed no significant abnormalities.

Physical Treatment Plan

Bed rest with knees and hips in moderate flexion was recommended, along with a trial of either cold compresses or warm moist compresses p.r.n. for pain relief.

Comment

This patient with an acute lumbosacral strain, without neurological evidence of disc disease, is put in a rest position to avoid stress to her back. A trial of either superficial cold or superficial heat (as there is considerable variability in individual response) is made for pain relief. The prognosis in the absence of neurological changes is usually favorable and the patient can be treated at home. When symptoms subside sufficiently, she will be referred to physical therapy for instruction in avoidance of back trauma and exercises to mobilize the lumbar fascia and stretch the hamstrings.

References
Efficacy of heat and cold.[1-6]
Bed rest and position.[12-14]
Back and hamstring exercises.[14]

b. Recurrent lumbosacral strain and discogenic disease

The patient returns two years later with a history of only mild, intermittent pain associated with heavy lifting or sleeping on an excessively soft mattress. For the past two weeks the pain has been severe, aggravated by prolonged sitting (especially driving), bending, and particularly stooping. On examination there is moderate restriction of lumbar flexion and tenderness of the lumbosacral juncture on the right. The neurological examination and straight leg raising tests are within normal limits. The right leg is noted to be three-quarters of an inch shorter than the left. X-rays show narrowing of the L-5, S-1 interspace with anterior osteophytes.

Physical Treatment Plan

This patient with recurrent lumbosacral strain and lumbar disc degeneration will be treated with hot compresses for pain relief. She will be fitted with a firm corset. A three-eighths-inch heel lift on the right shoe will be provided. She will be advised to obtain a firm "orthopedic" mattress, and will be referred to a physical therapist for exercises to mobilize her lumbar fascia and her hamstring muscles and to strengthen her abdominal muscles. In addition, she will be taught methods to lie, sit, and stand, to move from lying to sitting to standing, and to lift in such a way as to minimize back stress.

Comment

The patient has a chronic recurrent lumbosacral strain and will obtain relief during exacerbations from warm compresses and partial immobilization of the lumbar spine during activities by means of a corset. A firm mattress, care to avoid strain on her back, as well as obtaining maximal mobilization of her lumbar fascia and hamstrings, will offer added protection as she has a chronic condition and further trouble can be anticipated over the years.

References
Braces and corsets.[15,16]
Shoe modifications.[15]
Assistive devices.[17]

c. Acute lumbar disc

The patient is seen five years later with a history of severe pain in the back radiating to the buttocks, posterior thigh and calf on the right, precipitated by bending over to pull weeds. The pain has been severe enough to preclude walking. On examination, the significant findings in addition to the painful back are a diminished ankle jerk on the right and weakness on attempting to dorsiflex the right foot. X-rays reveal further narrowing in the L-5, S-1 interspace.

Physical Treatment Plan

Because of the evidence of neurological (radicular) involvement, this patient should be hospitalized and orthopedic or neurosurgical consultation should be obtained.

Comment

There is no convincing evidence of a specific effect of pelvic traction in relieving lumbar disc compression syndromes, although pain relief apparently attributable to stretching lumbar muscles is often obtained. Pelvic traction may be prescribed on occasion when it serves to keep a patient in bed.

References

Pelvic traction.[12,13,18,19]

3. Problem: Ankylosing Spondylitis

The patient is a 24-year-old male with a history of recurrent low back and buttock pain for the past year and a half. At times the pain has been disabling and in the past few weeks the patient has been in rather severe distress. He has noted considerable improvement since he was given indomethacin. The significant findings are marked restriction of lumbar motion, moderate atrophy of the paralumbar muscles, a chest expansion of one-and-a-half inches, and slight restriction of rotation and flexion of the cervical spine. X-rays reveal typical destructive changes in both sacroiliac joints and syndesmophytes in the lumbar spine.

Physical Treatment Plan

This patient should be referred to physical therapy for exercises to maintain mobility in the cervical spine, increase chest expansion, maximize extension of the spine, and to maintain mobility in the hips. He should be taught to lie prone for at least one hour daily. He should be given a small, firm pillow, or preferably should use no pillow, in order to minimize neck flexion. He should have a firm mattress and be taught postural positioning to avoid flexion deformities in the neck, back, and hips. A warm shower in the morning to facilitate limbering up, exercises and the use of a pool for stretching, and general conditioning exercises are advised.

Comment

Essentially, this disorder poses a lifetime problem. Although the young man has no complications at this time, it is generally advisable to have the patient seen in consultation with a rheumatologist or other physician experienced in the management of this disorder.

References

British Rheumatism Association ankylosing spondylitis back protection pamphlet.[20]

4. Problem: Osteoporotic Spine

The patient is a 73-year-old female who developed spontaneous onset of pain in the mid-dorsal area three days ago. The pain has been persistent and is aggravated by bending, twisting, and coughing. There is local tenderness over the spinous process at the eighth dorsal vertebra. X-rays reveal severe osteoporosis of the entire spine with 50 percent compression of the eighth dorsal vertebra. There are no neurological deficits.

Physical Treatment Plan

Although this appears to be senile osteoporosis with a spontaneous compression fracture, the patient should be hospitalized and investigated carefully for any other cause of either the osteoporosis or the vertebral compression fracture. In the absence of neurological findings, the following are ordered: a full lumbodorsal corset with rigid stays, a firm mattress, and a referral to the physical therapist for instruction in avoidance of back strain and maintenance of posture by bed and chair positioning during the acute phase. Back extension exercises will be added along with increasing sitting and walking endurance, when tolerated, during the convalescent phase. Ambulation should be encouraged early to prevent deconditioning and circulatory stasis.

Comment

Although this is an acute process, most patients are benefited by superficial warm, moist compresses as adjunctive therapy to relieve pain. In the acute phase (first two weeks), a repetitive search for evidence of spinal cord dysfunction must be made.

References

Corset.[15,16]

5. Problem: Benign Fibrositis

The patient is a 57-year-old female who, for the last 15 years, has suffered from a rather chronic, recurrent stiffness and aching about her neck, shoulders, and back. This is particularly aggravated by damp weather, chilling, and fatigue. On examination she has minimal restriction of motion of the cervical spine and essentially normal motion in the lumbar spine, shoulders, hips, and peripheral joints. Laboratory and x-ray examinations are within normal limits.

Physical Treatment Plan

The management of this problem consists of superficial heat to the affected areas, posture training (including sitting posture), attention to proper mattress, and referral to a physical therapist for instruction in general limbering up routine and a physical conditioning exercise program.

Comment

Fibrositis is a benign chronic condition for which symptomatic physical measures and analgesics will be useful to minimize the patient's discomfort. Occasional patients are benefited by the use of methyl salicylate as a topical ointment, or by kneading massage over particularly painful areas. An occasional patient obtains additional symptomatic benefit from the use of local diathermy for particularly persistent focal areas of tenderness. Warm (woolen) clothing and avoidance of drafts and chilling is helpful to minimize exacerbations.

References
Posture.[20]
Exercise.[14,20]

6. Problem: Shoulder Pain
a. Acute tendinitis-bursitis shoulder
This 45-year-old woman developed severe pain in the right shoulder after vigorous spring cleaning. On examination the patient seemed to be carefully cradling her painful right arm to avoid motion. There is minimal shoulder motion objectively because of painful guarding. There is marked tenderness about the shoulder, particularly on the lateral aspect in the region of the greater tuberosity. X-rays reveal no calcifications or abnormalities in the shoulder joint.

Physical Treatment Plan
In addition to analgesic medication, physical management will consist of a forearm supporting sling and ice packs to the shoulder area.

Comment
This patient has acute tendinitis in the right shoulder and has too much pain to attempt to mobilize the joint. She will probably obtain partial pain relief from ice packs, although a few patients will prefer moist warm compresses.

b. Subacute tendinitis-bursitis shoulder
After five days the pain has subsided and the patient spontaneously moves her arm, although it is still very painful.

Physical Treatment Plan
At this subacute phase, the patient is referred to the physical therapist for gentle mobilization. The sling is discontinued.

Comment
Early mobilization within pain tolerance is essential to minimize contracture of the shoulder.

c. Chronic shoulder pain and contracture

The same patient is seen again four weeks later, at which time she has mild-to-moderate, persistent, chronic pain in the region of the shoulder. This pain is particularly aggravated by raising the arm against gravity. She lacks about 20 degrees of abduction, forward flexion, and internal and external rotation.

Physical Treatment Plan

Physical therapy will be continued with more aggressive and frequent stretching activities, to be conducted both in supervised therapy and in the home program.

Comment

This patient initially developed acute tendinitis or bursitis in the right shoulder necessitating immobilization and protection (sling) with cold compresses. Gradual mobilization and hot compresses were added as her condition improved. It is imperative that this problem receive supervision from a physical therapist so that the patient will not be left with a chronic contracture of the shoulder capsule. When the pain subsides sufficiently, resistive exercises should be added to the regimen to increase strength and endurance.

References

Exercises to mobilize acute, subacute, and chronic shoulder problems.[21]
Heat and cold modalities.[1-6]

7. Problem: "Tennis Elbow"

The patient is a 37-year-old businessman who plays tennis regularly and enthusiastically on weekends. For the past few months he has had increasing pain and discomfort in the region of his elbow, especially with his back-hand strokes. The pain became rather severe two days ago after he participated in a tennis tournament. On examination there is exquisite tenderness over the right lateral epicondyle. Resisting wrist extension exacerbates his discomfort. X-rays are within normal limits.

Physical Treatment Plan

Elbow rest, ice packs during the first day or two of acute pain; then a hinged elbow support splint will be worn, particularly when playing tennis and during other stressful activities, to minimize trauma.

Comment

Epicondylitis is a very common problem and tends to be recurrent. It is often relieved by splints that avoid excessive stress to the elbow. Local steroids are frequently very successful in alleviating persistent symptoms and an occasional chronic problem will respond to a course of diathermy, including ultrasound to the elbow, three to five times a week for two or three weeks.

References
Elbow splints.[15]
Heat, cold, and diathermy.[1-6]

8. Problem: Acute Septic Arthritis in the Wrist

A 16-year-old female has a history of migrating arthritis of two days' duration with persistent and increasing pain in the left wrist. This has been associated with chills, scattered small vesicular lesions on the face, trunk, and arms, and a vaginal discharge positive for gonorrhea on smear and culture. X-rays reveal only soft-tissue swelling. Synovial fluid aspirated from the wrist is purulent and the culture is positive for gonococci.

Physical Treatment Plan

Treatment in addition to antibiotic therapy consists of a plaster of paris splint to the left wrist and cold compresses. As inflammation and pain subside over the next few days, the splint is removed, hot compresses are applied, and assisted range of motion exercises are begun, progressing to active exercise until range of motion is restored.

Comment

This patient has acute gonorrheal arthritis, which is diagnosed early and will respond well to antibiotic therapy. The physical management is designed to relieve pain by immobilization and cold compresses, and then to begin gently with active exercise to minimize any possibility of a contracture or deformity developing. Splinting should be performed with the wrist in the neutral position or in slight dorsiflexion. An active exercise program should be avoided until acute inflammatory signs have subsided. After one or two days of antibiotic therapy, warm moist compresses may be more comfortable for the patient, particularly when applied just prior to attempting gentle range of motion exercise. Cold compresses can be administered with the wrist resting on an ice pack. The use of a sling as a supplemental immobilizing aid during the acute phase may give additional pain relief.

References
Wrist splints.[22]

9. Problem: Generalized Osteoarthritis

A 51-year-old female complains of moderate pain in the distal interphalangeal joints of the fingers of both hands and the proximal interphalangeal joints of the right second and third fingers. The pain first began six months ago. Occasionally, she has had mildly painful joint swelling in the left knee. Examination reveals typical Heberden's nodes in the distal interphalangeal joints and Bouchard's nodes in the proximal inter-phalangeal joints of the second and third fingers of the right hand. There is a palpable fluid wave and mild joint margin tenderness in the left knee. There is no loss of knee motion.

Physical Treatment Plan

Paraffin soaks for pain relief to the hands are prescribed, as well as hot compresses, soaks, or paraffin painted on the left knee. During the exacerbation of pain in the knee, a cane is used in the right hand to provide additional joint protection. The patient is referred to the physical therapist for instructions about fitting and using a cane, for a quadriceps strengthening program, and for exercises to maintain range of motion in the fingers.

Comment

This patient has a chronic painful disorder that usually is slowly progressive, waxing and waning for varying periods of time. Physical therapy may use hot paraffin to relieve pain, although many patients will benefit from just soaking their hands in warm water. The patient should be referred to an occupational therapist for instruction in techniques to protect her finger joints during her daily activities and thereby minimize pain and deforming stresses. The painful knee results in inhibition of the quadriceps muscle. The weak quadriceps does not allow for normal knee function and for the protection that intact musculature provides. There is little risk of a knee contracture developing in this mild noninflammatory disorder.

References
Paraffin.[23]
Cane gait.[17,24]
Quadriceps strengthening exercise.[25,26]

10. Problem: Rheumatoid Arthritis and Psoriasis
a. Early-insidious

A 26-year-old housewife with psoriasis and rheumatoid arthritis first presented with an insidious onset of multiple joint pains, swelling, and stiffness, primarily affecting the proximal interphalangeal and metacarpophalangeal joints in the hands, right wrist, and both knees.

Physical Treatment Plan

A program of rest, consisting of a two-hour nap in the afternoon and eight to ten hours of sleep at night, is implemented. The patient will be referred to occupational therapy for instructions in joint protection and work simplification. A static wrist-stabilizing splint for daytime use and posterior long-leg night splints to maintain the knees in full extension are ordered. The patient will be given exercises twice daily to maintain range of motion in the affected joints. She will be given a firm mattress and instructed to use a small head pillow. No pillows will be permitted under her knees, and she will be taught to lie prone for at least one hour daily in order to prevent hip flexion contractures. A hot bath or shower in the morning and evening, and paraffin or hot water soaks for her hands will help relieve pain and stiffness. Her major exercise program, which is designed to achieve a maximum range of motion to all affected joints (as opposed to limbering up from morning stiffness), should be performed at mid-day, when morning stiffness is at a minimum and before fatigue has begun.

Comment

This patient with psoriasis and rheumatoid arthritis has no deformity. On a conservative regimen, deformity may be prevented and satisfactory pain relief obtained. Although certain drugs are contraindicated in psoriasis, the physical treatment plan is not altered by the presence or absence of coexistent psoriasis with rheumatoid arthritis. A wrist-stabilizing splint will minimize trauma to the joint during use and is usually an effective measure for relieving wrist pain in rheumatoid arthritis. If her response is prompt, further referral may be unnecessary.

References
Range of motion exercises.[27,28]
Paraffin.[23]
Bed rest.[29]
Wrist splint.[22,30]

b. Early-progressive
Over the next two months the patient developed progressive pain, stiffness, and early subluxations in the right wrist and in the metacarpophalangeal joints of both hands. X-rays showed soft-tissue swelling and early erosions at the joint margins of the metacarpophalangeal joints and of the right wrist.

Physical Treatment Plan
Hospitalization and rheumatological consultation.

Comment
Progressive joint destruction and unremitting pain are indications for more aggressive therapy. Consultation at this time may be of great value.

11. Problem: Chronic Deforming Rheumatoid Arthritis
A 53-year-old, depressed, chronically ill male with rheumatoid arthritis associated with high titer rheumatoid factor and subcutaneous nodules on the elbows has marked deformity in both hands with typical ulnar deviation of the metacarpophalangeal joints, swan-neck deformities in the fingers, moderate restriction of elbow and shoulder motion, and moderate

contractures of the knees. His course has been persistent with evidence both clinically and radiologically of relentless joint destruction.

Physical Treatment Plan
The patient should be referred for consultation to a rheumatologist and an orthopedist for planning subsequent management.

Comment
Referral to a rehabilitation center may be essential to provide the multiple services necessary to determine the physical, medical, psychological, social, and surgical aspects of this patient's management. Although he has severe deforming arthritis, it may be that, with medical control of his painful inflammatory disease, the deformed joints will function adequately and surgical intervention avoided or required only for a few joints.

References
Hand deformities in rheumatoid arthritis.[31]

12. Problem: Subacute Rheumatoid Knee
The same patient returns for follow-up three months after having received treatment in a rehabilitation center. Although he is generally improved, he has recently noted increased pain in the right knee associated with swelling, heat, and mild redness. Aspiration of the knee revealed no evidence of infection, and x-rays are unchanged. The knee lacks 10 degrees of extension. His disease is otherwise under adequate control.

Physical Treatment Plan
A resting posterior-molded splint for the right leg, extending from the upper thigh to the bottom of the foot, is prescribed to relieve pain and maintain extension in the knee. Isometric quadriceps strengthening exercises for the knees will be done twice daily following active range of motion to the knees to improve strength and mobility. Crutches are used during the flare-up to protect the knee. The patient is referred to the physical therapist for a review of his exercises, for instruction in crutch gait, and for consideration of platform crutches because of the extensive hand, wrist, and elbow deformities.

Comment
This patient has a chronic, severe problem, but careful attention to details of management in conjunction with appropriate specialist referral can maintain function and minimize discomfort.

References
Crutch gait and platform crutches.[17,24]
Posterior molded splints.[22,32-34]

Range of motion exercises.[27,28]
Isometric quadriceps exercise in rheumatoid arthritis.[25,26]

13. Problem: Degenerative Joint Disease of the Hip
a. Acute exacerbation of hip pain

A 53-year-old male attorney is seen because of complaints of pain in the left buttock and groin for the past two years. These pains have become severe since he slipped on a loose rug a week ago. Examination reveals marked pain and restriction of motion in the left hip and x-rays show mild hip degenerative changes.

Physical Treatment Plan

Bed rest and home visits from a physical therapist are arranged to instruct the patient in a non-weight-bearing crutch gait for protection of the left hip. Hot packs are to be administered for pain relief and to relax muscles prior to assisted range of motion in the hip. The patient is encouraged to maintain a prone position for at least one hour daily to prevent hip flexion contractures.

Comment

Although the underlying hip joint process is a chronic one, this is an acute exacerbation. Despite the relative acuteness, warm moist compresses are usually effective for hip pain relief and an occasional patient may benefit from diathermy even at this stage.

b. Chronic hip pain

One week later, the pain at rest has subsided and hip motion in now 75 percent normal. The patient has pain at the extremes of his range of hip motion and on weight bearing. A one-inch shortening of the left leg is noted.

Physical Treatment Plan

Patient will continue graduated exercises to increase range of motion in the hip. In addition, strengthening exercises for the hip muscles will be permitted and partial weight bearing on crutches can now be tolerated. His home will be evaluated for hazards by a visiting therapist (physical therapist or occupational therapist) and an assessment made of the need for removal of slippery rugs and placement of grab bars for safety and to minimize stress on moving to and from the toilet. His daily activities, including dressing, will be reviewed with the objective of minimizing stress to the hip. With the rapid rate of improvement he has shown so far, it can be assumed that he will soon be ready to progress from crutches to a cane. Attention should be given to modification of his shoes to compensate for a one-inch shortening of the leg.

Comment

The patient has a chronic underlying degenerative hip joint problem, but the acute exacerbation is subsiding and he is rapidly returning to his previous level of function. The emphasis is on joint protection with crutches and cane to minimize joint stress, and maintenance of hip mobility and strength through an exercise program.

c. Severe chronic painful hip

Two years later the same patient returns with a history of progressive pain in the left hip and an increasing limp, despite continuing therapy. Examination reveals moderate atrophy of the hip musculature and reduction of range of motion in the left hip to 50 percent of normal. X-rays show marked progression of degenerative changes in the hip joint.

Physical Treatment Plan

A referral to an orthopedist for further management is recommended. (See Chapter 8.)

References

Leg length, shoe corrections.[15]
Cane-crutch gait.[17,24]
Assistive devices (grab bar for toilet).[24,35]
Hip exercises.[26-28]

14. Problem: Acute Gout, Left Ankle

A 32-year-old male was awakened two days ago with severe pain in the left ankle. The pain is unrelenting, and weight bearing is almost intolerable. The ankle is markedly swollen, erythematous, and exquisitely tender. X-rays are within normal limits; the serum uric acid is 9 mg percent. Aspiration of the ankle joint reveals typical monosodium urate crystals. Drug therapy is initiated. (See Chapter 6.)

Physical Treatment Plan

The patient is given a regimen of bed rest and a trial of cold compresses p.r.n. for pain relief. Instruction by a physical therapist in a non-weight-bearing crutch gait is ordered.

Comment

The acute gouty episode is self-limited and of short duration with proper therapy. During the acute episode, physical measures other than rest are of little value, and hot compresses or deep heat will usually aggravate the condition. The patient will need crutches for ambulation for the two to three days required to bring the attack under good control. Exercise therapy is not necessary as the attack is self-limited and complete recovery in the early cases is anticipated.

References
Non-weight-bearing crutch gait.[17,24]

15. Problem: Reiter's Syndrome with Persistent Heel and Ankle (hind foot) Pain

The patient is a 24-year-old male with a history of urethritis, conjunctivitis, and pain and swelling in the right knee, beginning two months previously. For the past three weeks he has had persistent pain and swelling in the left ankle and pain in the right heel on weight bearing. The positive findings on examination at this time are confined to the left ankle, which is moderately swollen and tender, and to the right heel, which reveals marked tenderness on deep pressure over the anterior aspect of the distal calcaneus. The only laboratory abnormality is a sedimentation rate of 25 mm per hour. X-ray shows soft-tissue swelling about the left ankle and an irregular pereosteal reaction on the anterior aspect of the right calcaneus.

Physical Treatment Plan

The following measures are prescribed: hot soaks for both feet in a tub or whirlpool; active range of motion exercises to the left ankle, three to five times a day, to attempt achieving the maximum tolerated range; referral to a physical therapist for training in an alternating crutch gait designed to protect both lower extremities; referral to a podiatrist for shoe modification to cushion the right heel.

Comment

Although Reiter's syndrome is generally a self-limited disease, persistence of pain in the heels and ankles can be disabling when the patient is otherwise essentially recovered. Attention is focused on pain relief with the crutch gait and shoe modifications. Consideration may have to be given to orthopedic referral for a short leg brace to relieve pain and permit functional ambulation. Warm soaks for pain relief prior to exercise are a useful adjunct and help facilitate the range of motion exercises, which are prescribed to minimize deforming contracture in the left ankle.

References
BKBB brace.[36]
Crutch gait.[17,24]
Shoe corrections.[15]
Ankle exercises.[27,28]

16. Problem: Juvenile Rheumatoid Arthritis with Chronic Elbow and Forefoot Arthritis

The patient is an eight-year-old girl with a nine-month history of intermittent swelling in the left knee, associated with pain on walking. She has also had some stiffness in the left elbow. On examination she appears mildly chronically ill. At this time she has no evidence of pain, swelling, or limitation of motion in her knees. However, the left elbow appears to be slightly swollen and lacks 10 degrees of extension. The metacarpophalangeal joints are slightly tender and the patient avoids stepping off her toes when walking. X-rays of all affected joints are normal. The rheumatoid factor is normal. A Wintrobe sedimentation rate is 25 mm per hour.

Physical Treatment Plan

Active and assistive range of motion exercise for the left elbow is prescribed, along with range of motion exercises for other joints if they become involved. The patient will be referred to a podiatrist for metatarsal pads to be placed in her shoes just proximal to the metatarsophalangeal joints. This will relieve pressure on those joints in walking. She will be referred to a physical therapist for preventive range of motion exercises and gait instruction (pain permitting). Further pediatric rheumatological consultation should be obtained because the systemic complications of juvenile rheumatoid arthritis can be severe.

Comment

Elbow contractures are very difficult to reverse, and every effort to prevent them should be made. Stretching the elbow forcibly will usually aggravate the condition. Gentle assisted range of motion exercises (three to five gentle stretches two or three times a day) preceded by hot compresses or soaks will usually give the best results. A carefully balanced program must be designed to permit as normal a life-style as possible without undue joint stress.

References
Shoe, metatarsal pad.[15]
Elbow exercise.[28]

C. Summary

The physician must use the most direct therapy to achieve the goals of pain relief, prevention of deformity, and restoration of function. These goals can be achieved in the vast majority of patients with articular disorders through simple regimens using readily available equipment and by procedures suitable for home therapy. Where progress is unsatisfactory or extensive and relentless disease is present, early appropriate consultation or referral to a rehabilitation center will minimize suffering and disability.

REFERENCES

1. Fountain, F. P., Gersten, J. W., and Sengir, O.: Decrease in muscle spasm produced by ultrasound, hot packs, and infrared radiation, Arch. Phys. Med. 41:293, July 1960.

2. Cordray, Y. M. and Krusen, E. M., Jr.: Use of hydrocollator packs in the treatment of neck and shoulder pains, Arch. Phys. Med. 40:105, March 1959.

3. Lehman, J. F., Brunner, G. D., and Stow, R. W.: Pain threshold measurements after therapeutic application of ultrasound, microwaves and infrared, Arch. Phys. Med. 39:560, September 1958.

4. Abramson, D. et al.: Comparison of wet and dry heat in raising temperature of tissues, Arch. Phys. Med. 48:654, December 1967.

5. Kirk, J. A. and Kersley, G. D.: Heat and cold in the physical treatment of rheumatoid arthritis of the knee: a controlled clinical trial, Ann. Phys. Med. 9:270, 1967-68.

6. Fischer, E. and Solomon, S.: Physiological responses to heat and cold. In Therapeutic Heat, ed. S. Licht, New Haven, Elizabeth Licht, 1965.

7. Martin, G. M. and Corbin, K. B.: An evaluation of conservative treatment for patients with cervical disk syndrome, Arch. Phys. Med. 35:87, February 1954.

8. British Association of Physical Medicine: Pain in the neck and arm: a multicentre trial of the effects of physiotherapy, Brit. Med. J. 1:253, January 29, 1966.

9. Colachis, S. C., Jr. and Strohm, B. R.: A study of tractive forces and angle of pull on vertebral interspaces in the cervical spine, Arch. Phys. Med. 46:820, December 1965.

10. Swaim, L. T.: The orthopedic and physical therapeutic treatment of chronic arthritis, JAMA 103:1589, November 24, 1934.

11. Cailliet, R.: Neck and Arm Pain, Philadelphia, F. A. Davis Company, 1964, p. 81.

12. Judovich, B. D.: Lumbar traction therapy and dissipated force factors, J. Lancet 74:411, October 1954.

13. Ramsey, R. H.: Conservative treatment of intervertebral disk lesions. In The American Academy of Orthopaedic Surgeons Instructional Course Lectures, ed. the Program Committee on Instructional Courses, Vol. 11, 1954, pp. 118-120.

14. Ishmael, W. B. and Shorbe, H. B.: Care of the Back, Philadelphia, J. B. Lippincott, 1963.

15. Licht, S.: Orthotics, Baltimore, Waverly Press, 1966.

16. Norton, P. L. and Brown, T.: The immobilizing efficiency of back braces, J. Bone Joint Surg. 39-A:111, January 1957.

17. Lowman, E. W. and Klinger, J. L.: Aids to Independent Living, New York, McGraw-Hill, 1969.

18. Lehmann, J. F. and Brunner, G. D.: A device for the application of heavy lumbar traction: its mechanical effects, Arch. Phys. Med. 39:696, November 1958.

19. Semmes, R. E.: Ruptures of the Lumbar Intervertebral Disc, Springfield, Ill., Charles C Thomas, 1964, p. 27.

20. British Rheumatism Association: Ankylosing Spondylitis Pamphlet.

21. Cailliet, R.: Shoulder Pain, Philadelphia, F. A. Davis Company, 1966.

22. Ehrlich, G. E.: Rest and splinting. In Total Management of the Arthritic Patient, Philadelphia, J. B. Lippincott, 1973, pp. 47-59.

23. Harris, R. and Millard, J. B.: Paraffin-wax baths in the treatment of rheumatoid arthritis, Ann. Rheum. Dis. 14:278, September 1955.

24. *Sorenson, L., Ulrich, P. G., Coles, C. L., and Grendahl, B. C.:* Ambulation, A Manual for Nurses, *Rehabilitation Publication No. 707, Minneapolis, American Rehabilitation Foundation.*

25. *Machover, S. and Sapecky, A. J.: Effect of isometric exercise on the quadriceps muscle in patients with rheumatoid arthritis,* Arch. Phys. Med. 47:737, November 1966.

26. *Magness, J. L., Lillegard, C., Sorenson, S., and Winkowski, P.: Isometric strengthening of hip muscles using a belt,* Arch. Phys. Med. 52:158, April 1971.

27. *Swezey, R. L.: Exercises with a beach ball for increasing range of joint motion,* Arch. Phys. Med. 48:253, May 1967.

28. *The Arthritis Foundation:* Simple Exercise, The Helping Hand, Diet Guide.

29. *Mills, J. A.: Value of bed rest in patients with rheumatoid arthritis,* New Eng. J. Med. 284:453, March 4, 1971.

30. *Gault, S. J. and Spyker, J. M.: Beneficial effect of immobilization of joints in rheumatoid and related arthritides: a splint study using sequential analysis,* Arthritis Rheum. 12:34, February 1969.

31. *Swezey, R. L.: Approaches to deformities in rheumatoid arthritis,* Postgrad. Med. 45:136, January 1969.

32. *Harris, R. and Copp, E. P.: Immobilization of the knee joint in rheumatoid arthritis,* Ann. Rheum. Dis. 21:353, 1962.

33. *Fried, D. M.: Splints for arthritis. In* Arthritis and Physical Medicine, *ed. S. Licht, New Haven, Elizabeth Licht, 1969, pp. 285-314.*

34. *Conference on Criteria for and Evaluation of Orthopedic Measures in the Management of Deformities of Rheumatoid Arthritis: Evaluations of splinting,* Arthritis Rheum. 7:585, 1964.

35. *MacBain, K. P.:* Aids and Adaptations, *Toronto, The Canadian Arthritis & Rheumatism Society.*

36. *Bowers, J. A. and Klassen, E. G.: Use of short leg braces with patellar tendon bearing cuffs,* Arch. Phys. Med. 46:436, June 1965.

CHAPTER 6

Guidelines for the Selection and Use of Drugs in Arthritis

Norman O. Rothermich, M.D., F.A.C.P.
Clinical Professor of Medicine
The Ohio State University
Columbus, Ohio

Medical Director
Columbus Medical Center Research Foundation

CHAPTER 6

| Guidelines for the
| Selection and
| Use of Drugs in Arthritis
| *Norman O. Rothermich, M.D., F.A.C.P.*

A. Introduction

Since 1949, research has provided the practitioner with a growing number of useful drugs for the management of various arthritic disorders. Many of these drugs have the potential for significant benefit in controlling symptoms and disability; however, they also pose the potential threat of significant adverse reactions.

As a practical guide for selecting and using available drugs, it is a good general principle to start with the safest effective drug at the smallest dosage that will achieve a desirable result. Since drug tolerance can vary widely from patient to patient, there is no way of predicting in any given patient the effective and tolerable dose. This specific dose can only be determined by starting at a low level and gradually increasing to a practical effective therapeutic level, with a predetermined maximum level. Of course, these are general principles for drug therapy in most diseases, but they are perhaps more applicable to antirheumatic drugs than to any other.

The philosophy regarding dosage should be carried over to the selection of drugs in the treatment of arthritis. It is patently absurd to treat a new mild case of rheumatoid arthritis with corticosteroids or cyclophosphamide as the initial therapy. The safest, most innocuous drugs with some degree of effectiveness should be employed first in the treatment of any arthritis. With persistence of disease activity, step-ups in a graduated fashion can be made, employing drugs that are more potent, though perhaps more toxic. This philosophy should apply, even when it may be necessary at the very outset to use potent drugs. Start with the safest effective drug at the smallest dosage that will achieve a desirable result.

This chapter will offer the practitioner an overview of the commonly used drugs, presented in the general sequence of relative potency. The following figure illustrates the general principle of beginning with the safest measures before proceeding to drugs that offer the potential for greater therapeutic effectiveness and hazardous side effects.

Flow Sheet for Drug Therapy in Rheumatoid Arthritis

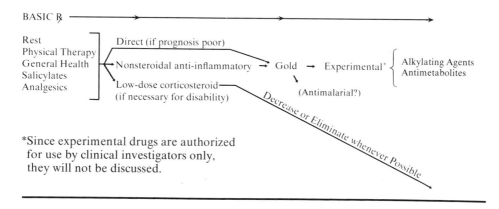

*Since experimental drugs are authorized for use by clinical investigators only, they will not be discussed.

This flow sheet was designed to provide the practitioner with a dynamic concept of drug therapy in rheumatoid arthritis. It is emphasized that the basic therapeutic program of rest, physical therapy, etc. continues uninterrupted. To this basic program is added the nonsteroidal anti-inflammatory drugs and/or chrysotherapy. It is not unreasonable to expect a high control rate with the appropriate use of all possible drug therapies.

B. Basic Therapy

As mentioned earlier, practitioners should begin a management program with a basic therapeutic approach that includes rest, physical therapy, attention to general health, salicylates, and analgesics. Chapter 5 offers numerous aids in making effective use of rest and physical therapy. Chapter 4 presents practical guidelines for using salicylates and analgesics. This chapter will focus on drugs that offer higher therapeutic potential and, of course, higher levels of risk.

C. Nonsteroidal Anti-Inflammatory Compounds

Certain chemicals have been discovered, some with perhaps a degree of serendipity, that have a potent anti-inflammatory effect in animals, and an antirheumatic action in humans. The term antirheumatic is used in a general sense and indicates that the drug has a beneficial effect in human rheumatic disease, but the precise action in producing this antirheumatic effect is not entirely clear. It may or may not be related to the anti-inflammatory effect demonstrated in animals.

1. Indomethacin*

Indomethacin has been available for clinical use since the middle 1960s. Its discovery resulted from research into tryptophan metabolism in rheumatoid arthritis and the role of indole derivatives.

a. Indications

We have found that indomethacin can produce a striking benefit in about 25 percent of cases of rheumatoid arthritis, and worthwhile improvement in an additional 25 percent. As yet, we have no way of predicting which two of four patients will get a good effect and which two will not. Because of the striking benefit in the one patient in four, as well as the worthwhile improvement in one additional patient, it would seem appropriate that in every patient with rheumatoid arthritis who has failed to respond to the basic program including adequate salicylates, and who does not have compelling reasons for chrysotherapy, a trial with indomethacin should be undertaken.

Our experiences seem to indicate that indomethacin often provides dramatic relief of pain and disability in severe osteoarthritis of the hip. The reason for this dramatic benefit is not entirely clear because the hip disease seems to be unchanged, and often progresses to ultimate destruction. The drug, however, may control the hip symptoms quite adequately to permit ambulation and little disability for periods of up to several years. The drug is not approved for use in other forms of osteoarthritis.

We have found indomethacin to be highly effective in the treatment of ankylosing spondylitis that has not responded adequately to conventional doses of aspirin. It has been our experience that effective control may be obtained with as little as 50 mg daily.

*Publisher's Note: Please refer to prescribing information available from the manufacturer for a complete presentation of contraindications, warnings, precautions, adverse reactions, and dosage.

Indomethacin has proven beneficial in acute gout and, in our opinion, it is about equal in effect to phenylbutazone.

b. Limitations

Indomethacin is contraindicated in children fourteen years or under, pregnant women, nursing mothers, patients with active gastrointestinal lesions or with a history of recurrent gastrointestinal lesions, and patients who are allergic to aspirin or indomethacin.

We have found that indomethacin has two principal side effects—gastric irritation with occasional ulcer formation, and cerebral effects in the form of headaches, dizziness, light-headedness, and, in highly susceptible individuals, some disturbance of sensorium.

In our practice, the CNS side effects are not considered a serious medical problem in that they have not had a residual effect, and usually disappear promptly upon withdrawal of the drug. Infrequently, we have found that the sense of disturbed equilibrium may make it difficult for the individual to function properly, such as operating machinery or driving an automobile. It appears that the CNS side effects are largely dose-related, but there is great individual variation in susceptibility.

In addition to the CNS side effects, indomethacin causes irritation of the stomach with ulcerogenic potential. We feel that the magnitude of risk is about the same as phenylbutazone, and not dissimilar to that with high-dose aspirin therapy. In our original investigations, gastric side effects presented a distressing problem, but they have been mitigated to a very great extent by the practice of giving the drug with meals or with milk. The bedtime dose, especially, should be taken with a large glass of milk. With this type of regimen, gastric complications, when they do occur, usually provide forewarning symptoms to the patient so that very early he may discontinue the drug or interrupt it temporarily. We have found that some patients can prevent gastric problems by taking the drug with an antacid.

An occasional patient in our practice will develop apparent bowel irritation with diarrhea which requires a reduction in dosage, temporary interruption, or even abandonment of the drug.

Very infrequently we have encountered a mildly pruritic macular dermatitis as a side effect. This has disappeared when we discontinued the drug. Other rare complications or side effects have been reported, but we have not found these to be a problem in our practice.

c. Dosage

In approved indications, except acute gouty arthritis, we usually start the drug at a low dosage of 25 mg twice daily, always given with meals, milk, or antacid. We increase the dosage by 25 mg once a week until the patient is taking 125 to 150 mg as a total daily dose.

This form of dosage schedule will allow many patients to build up to a tolerance to the drug so that the CNS side effects are minimized, whereas if a patient's initial dose is 125 mg daily, he may experience side effects to an intolerable degree.

We have also found that those who are going to respond well to indomethacin will do so within the first few days, although occasionally there may be a delay in benefit for as long as two or three weeks.

In acute gout, we use larger doses on a short-term basis. For example, we typically prescribe 50 mg every three to four hours up to a daily dose of 150 mg. The rapid subsidence of excrutiating pain and disability is, of course, quite gratifying.

2. Phenylbutazone*

Pyrazole derivatives have been in clinical use since the early 1950s. The first of these was phenylbutazone. A derivative, oxyphenbutazone, is so similar in its clinical profile that whatever is said about the former generally applies to the latter.

a. Indications

Phenylbutazone is highly effective in most of the so-called benign rheumatic diseases. These include osteoarthritis, spondylitis, gout, and the group of nonarticular inflammatory diseases commonly classified as bursitis, fibrositis, tendinitis, fasciitis, etc.

b. Limitations

Phenylbutazone has numerous side effects, the most serious of which is depression of the bone marrow. Any one or all elements can be depressed, and although occasionally we have found this to be an idiosyncratic action, most often it is a dose-related and sometimes slowly progressive effect. The problem is detectable by peripheral blood counts done at appropriate intervals. It is our practice to perform the blood tests at variable intervals, depending on dosage, with the higher dosages requiring tests at shorter intervals.

Phenylbutazone can cause significant sodium and fluid retention; therefore it should be given with caution to cardiac patients. Dermatitis, usually confined to a macular rash, has been a relatively rare occurrence in our practice.

---

*Publisher's Note: Please refer to prescribing information available from the manufacturer for a complete presentation of contraindications, warnings, precautions, adverse reactions, and dosage.

As with other drugs in this group, gastric irritation and peptic ulcer formation have been seen as rather common side effects. We have found that these problems can be sometimes obviated if the drug is taken with meals or milk at bedtime, or with an antacid. A capsule containing the drug and an alkalizing agent is available for patients who have gastric irritation from the drug.

c. Dosage

In accordance with the principles enunciated earlier in this chapter, we start the drug in low dosages, such as 100 mg, once or twice a day. When the drug first became available, recommendations were made for total daily doses as high as 800 mg. Now 400 mg should be considered the maximum daily dose.

In ankylosing spondylitis, we have found that 200 mg daily is usually sufficient to control the disease. In the acute phases of gout, we prescribe a daily dose of 100 mg every three or four hours for five doses.

D. Corticosteroids*

When cortisone was first introduced, it was thought to be the greatest boon of all time for the patient with rheumatoid arthritis. Within a few years, largely because of our own abuse and misuse of the drug, disillusionment set in. For a while, cortisone was even thought to be a curse to rheumatology. Of course, this was as wrong as the first reaction.

Corticosteroids should be neither absolutely proscribed nor excessively prescribed in rheumatic disease. Neither gross, wanton overdosage nor therapeutic nihilism can be considered acceptable, and both approaches should be deplored. In any discussion of the benefits and dangers of "cortisone therapy," the matter of dosage is of prime importance. It is helpful if a clear distinction is made between the high-dose therapy necessary for the more serious, and often fatal, rheumatic diseases and the very small, sometimes miniscule, doses to be used in the more benign rheumatic disorders.

Prednisone, in our practice, is the agent of choice for oral therapy. However, contrary to the general feeling that there is no difference between one analogue and another, some analogues do have certain advantages. It has been our observation that analogues of hydrocortisone may have unique peculiarities which in occasional clinical circumstances provide useful advantages. (See reference 5.)

*Publisher's Note: Please refer to prescribing information available from the manufacturer for a complete presentation of contraindications, warnings, precautions, adverse reactions, and dosage.

In certain few cases, where prednisone seems not to be as effective as expected, we have found it worthwhile to shift to one or another analogue to see if, at comparable dosage ranges, a better antirheumatic action can be achieved.

1. Limitations

Some practitioners are unduly fearful of the side effects of corticosteroids, whereas others are cavalier or unaware of them. A full knowledge and understanding of these side effects will allow the physician to adopt a balanced approach to steroid therapy.

Often in discussions of side effects, a clear distinction must be made between low and high dosages. For example, posterior subcapsular cataracts seem to have a causal relationship to long-term high-dose corticosteroid therapy, but not to lower dosage levels. Also, we have found that peptic ulceration is a rare complication of low-dose steroid therapy. In fact, the incidence has been lower than that of aspirin or the nonsteroidal antiinflammatory drugs in our practice.

It is our experience that at low dosage levels there has not been an impairment of wound healing or response to infection. Some of our patients who have been on low-dose steroid therapy for many years have undergone major surgery, such as total hip prosthesis, without difficulty. Healing and convalescence were not delayed. Of course, during the period of surgery, supplemental large doses of corticosteroids were given parenterally on the day of the operation and for several days thereafter in a gradually declining fashion.

It should be remembered that serious illness or injury produce the same burden on stress mechanisms as surgery, and should such physical trauma or acute febrile illness occur in a patient who is on long-term steroid therapy (or has been on it any time within the preceding year or year and a half) supplemental steroid therapy should be administered to him over the stressful period in much the same way as for surgical stress.

We have found that at the low-dose levels, psychic side effects are virtually unheard of. Even moon face and buffalo humping may appear temporarily and then recede. The two most distressing side effects of corticosteroids, even at low doses are:
   □ the effects on the skin of the forearms and forelegs, with marked atrophy and easy bruising (see illustration on following page). The skin may become so delicate that it shreds even on the slightest trauma. In some of our patients, this has required plastic grafts.

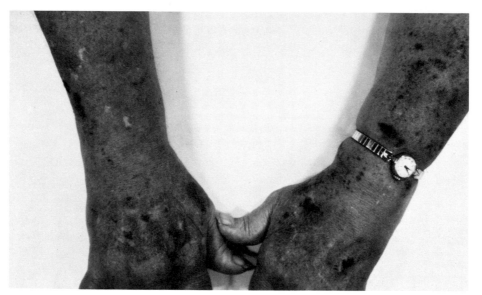

Shown above is an example of "easy bruising" in a 55-year-old female with rheumatoid arthritis who is receiving 8 mg methylprednisolone every other day.

□ osteoporosis, which can usually be regarded as an aggravation of a pre-existing tendency in postmenopausal women, in the elderly, and in patients with rheumatoid arthritis where osteoporosis is an integral part of the disease.

As a general rule, one which we have employed for more than 20 years, these patients on long-term corticosteroid therapy also receive an anticatabolic program.

2. Dosage

In the acutely ill patient with serious "collagen" rheumatic disease, we start prednisone in a dose of 10 mg, three or four times a day. Patients are instructed to take it with food or milk to prevent gastric ulceration. The higher the individual dose, the greater the hazard of ulcer formation. Even with the serious, and usually fatal diseases, we start at the lower dosage levels and build up as necessary, being constantly vigilant of the patient's critical condition and the rapidity of deterioration of the disease. When higher dosages are required, we use parenteral injection.

In rheumatoid arthritis, the total daily dose usually should not exceed 5 mg prednisone daily, and many of our patients have been returned to an adequate functional and productive state with doses as low as 1 mg two or three times a day. We make every effort to stay at 5 mg or less, and certainly do not exceed 7.5 mg daily for long-term maintenance. We have used 10 mg daily on a short-term basis.

We feel the key to successful steroid therapy in rheumatoid arthritis is to have both patient and physician jointly working together to reduce the dosage to the lowest level necessary to permit the patient to continue productive work and the basic activities of daily living. We give steroids to relieve disability, not to treat arthritis. We never regard them as substitutes for proper rest, physical therapy, salicylates, and all other forms of anti-rheumatic therapy.

Some clinicians advocate that all of the required corticosteroids be given in a single morning dose, not exceeding 7 to 10 mg on any maintenance basis. The objective is to mimic the body's natural physiology and avoid high levels of corticosteroid in the blood at other times of the day, especially in the evening. We question this rationale at the lower dosage levels. We have found that where the total daily dose is 5 mg or less, there is little or no interference with pituitary-adrenal function. Most of our patients find that the morning and evening doses of steroids provide more effective relief of disability. Some patients prefer smaller doses three or four times a day.

The alternate-day regimen, strongly recommended for other diseases, is not feasible in rheumatoid arthritis, in our judgment. Some rheumatologists, however, find it satisfactory and to their liking. There seems no doubt that pituitary-adrenal suppression is far less, if at all. It has been our experience, however, that alternate-day regimens do not prevent some of the distressing complications such as skin atrophy, easy bruising, moon face, buffalo hump, and probably osteoporosis.

We have also found that some of our patients on alternate-day regimens experience a "yo-yo" effect. On the steroid day they feel fine, but on the alternate day they may be virtually bedfast.

Systemic corticosteroids should be given only with great reluctance in disabling bursitis, tendinitis, fasciitis, shoulder periarthritis, etc. In other forms of arthritis (including psoriatic, Sjögren's, and others) the principles for the use of corticosteroids are much the same as in rheumatoid arthritis itself.

In polymyalgia rheumatica, we feel that systemic corticosteroids are virtually specific, and if the patient has prodromes of vision impairment, we give large doses, e.g., 30-60 mg prednisone per day. Because this disease occurs in the older age group, the dangers of osteoporosis and pathologic fractures are especially great with long-term therapy. It is our usual practice, therefore, to bring the maintenance dose to 5-10 mg daily within a few weeks.

117

If any visual disturbances recur, we raise the dosage quickly, and if necessary, use parenteral steroids. Temporal arteritis is an important feature of polymyalgia, and perhaps also arteritis occurring elsewhere in the body. We have found that arteritis in any form (such as periarteritis nodosa, Wegener's granulomatosis, hypersensitivity angiitis, and others in this category) is often an indication for the immediate use of systemic corticosteroids in quite high doses parenterally, e.g., 100-500 mg of prednisone daily. When the need for prednisone exceeds 30-40 mg daily we usually resort to parenteral administration, because we prefer to avoid large oral doses.

E. Chrysotherapy*

Gold salts have been used in the treatment of rheumatoid arthritis for more than 40 years. Perhaps because chrysotherapy has been the subject of considerable controversy throughout the years, many practitioners avoid it completely. Still, there is a voluminous literature, much of it favorable, and a general feeling among rheumatologists that chrysotherapy offers the patient with rheumatoid arthritis the best chance for a true drug-induced remission.

Viewed in the long perspective, chrysotherapy has a definite place in the management of rheumatoid arthritis. One of its big disadvantages is that it must be given by injection and its favorable results may not be apparent early in the course of therapy. In fact, in some cases, benefits may not be seen for three or four months, and, in some instances, even longer.

1. Limitations
The complication most feared by many physicians is bone marrow depression, yet this has been a very rare complication in our experience. Blood counts, performed at appropriate intervals, can often detect the bone marrow effect. We feel that a careful inquiry and search for purpuric spots is also essential.

Occasionally a patient will complain of feeling much worse for three or four days after each injection. It is our feeling that such a patient is probably having a "paradoxical reaction" and we usually discontinue the gold.

2. Dosage
Clinicians often ask: "When should gold therapy be started?" This is not an easy question to answer because once chrysotherapy is launched, the physician and patient are committed to continuing this program for extended

*Publisher's Note: Please refer to prescribing information available from the manufacturer for a complete presentation of contraindications, warnings, precautions, adverse reactions, and dosage.

periods if improvement occurs, or a minimum of 12-14 weeks even without benefit.

Sooner or later both will be haunted by the questions: "Was it really necessary in the first place?" and "Can it now be discontinued?"

We feel that most patients with rheumatoid arthritis should be given an opportunity on a basic program (discussed early in this chapter) and the addition of other temporizing measures. If these do not bring the disease into remission, or at least maintain the disease in adequate control, chrysotherapy should be considered. The more evidence there is of general active synovitis, the more urgent the need for chrysotherapy in our opinion.

The two forecasters of poor prognosis in our experience are rheumatoid nodules and a very high latex fixation titre. In the event that either one or both of these is present, we see a clear indication for early institution of chrysotherapy. If the disease shows relentless progression in the face of a good basic program and adequate suppressive measures, we begin chrysotherapy, even without the presence of nodules and a high latex titre.

It is customary to start with a "test dose" of only 10 mg. A week later, we give a 25-mg dose. The third and subsequent doses are at the 50-mg level. During this period we continue all other antirheumatic measures uninterrupted. When the beneficial effects of gold begin to appear, other measures, especially cortisone, are reduced and gradually eliminated.

Before each weekly injection, we question the patient intensively for any new unpleasant sensations, itching, or purplish blotches. If we detect any pruritic dermatitis, the gold is interrupted for several weeks until the dermatitis subsides and disappears. We resume treatment, but if the dermatitis returns, we again interrupt the gold therapy. On the third trial, we restart the gold at half the previous dose. Gold salts should never be injected in the presence of active gold dermatitis. Stomatitis is regarded in the same category as dermatitis, and we take the same therapeutic precautions.

Before each injection, we examine the urine for red blood cells and protein. If there are more than 10 RBC/hpf or more than 50 mg of albumin, we temporarily withhold gold injections until the urine becomes clear. If signs of renal toxicity again appear, we abandon therapy permanently. Blood counts are recommended by the manufacturers at every second weekly injection.

It is our practice to give the weekly injection until the patient shows a striking benefit or remission. At that point, we reduce the frequency, but not the amount of the injection until the patient may be receiving only one injection every three weeks for as long as the condition remains improved or in remission. Whenever flareups occur, the interval between injections is reduced to every two weeks or every week, if necessary. If a beneficial effect is not seen by the 20th week, the therapy should be considered ineffective and should not be reinstituted.

F. Antimalarial Therapy*

The use of chloroquine for rheumatoid arthritis was first introduced in the early 1950s, and, for a time, enjoyed some popularity. One theory held that chloroquine achieved a remission through a stabilization of the lysosomal membrane.

In the early 1960s, reports began to appear indicating that chloroquine was deposited in the pigmented tissues of the retina, chiefly around the macula, causing impairment of vision. As these reports increased, the drug was abandoned. It has since been replaced by hydroxychloroquine which is thought to be somewhat less toxic. It is my opinion that antimalarials should not occupy a regular place in the armamentarium against rheumatoid arthritis.

Despite the limitations mentioned, we feel that hydroxychloroquine is quite useful in certain cases of lupus erythematosus, especially those that are sun-sensitive. We employ a daily dose of 200 mg which is often sufficient for therapeutic benefit. We have not experienced retinal damage, but we arrange for an examination every three or four months by an ophthalmologist knowledgeable in chloroquine retinal deposits and the resulting type of "bull's eye" effect. Interruptions of therapy for two to three months have proven worthwhile in some cases.

G. Anti-Gout Drugs

This is not the place to discuss whether gout is the result of overproduction, underexcretion, or overconversion of uric acid. The fact is that in patients with gout, there is an enormous amount of urate in the total body pool—something like three or four times the normal level.

It should be understood that attempts to reduce the total body pool to the normal level have nothing to do directly with the treatment of acute

*Publisher's Note: Please refer to prescribing information available from the manufacturer for a complete presentation of contraindications, warnings, precautions, adverse reactions, and dosage.

inflammatory disease, or even the chronic polyarthritis of gout. In other words, if the patient is having an episode of acute podagra, it is needless, worthless, and possibly harmful to start drug therapy aimed at altering the total body pool of urate.

1. Uricosuric Agents*

Both patient and physician must understand that uricosuric therapy is a lifelong commitment, and is never to be interrupted. This is probably the most difficult aspect of managing the gout patient who is all too eager to dismiss his disease and put it out of his mind once the acute attack is over. I find it worthwhile to accompany uricosuric therapy with weight reduction, low-fat diet, and complete or nearly complete abstinence from alcohol.

There are many drugs that have a uricosuric effect, but the principal ones prescribed for gout are probenecid and sulfinpyrazone. Almost 100 percent of the urate is filtered through the glomerulus, and somewhere between 90 and 95 percent is reabsorbed in the tubule. The action of these two drugs is to block that reabsorption.

Probenecid has been in use longer and seems to have relatively few side effects. Dosage is usually initiated at 0.5 g daily in a divided dose. At the end of a week, the drug can be given at 0.5 g twice a day. If necessary, the daily dose can be increased by 0.5-g increments at monthly intervals until the patient is taking 2 g daily. It is generally unwise to bring about too abrupt a reduction of the serum urate level which may precipitate an acute attack.

Much the same can be said about sulfinpyrazone which is a highly potent and effective uricosuric drug with perhaps a higher incidence of side effects since it is a derivative of phenylbutazone. Doses can begin at 100 mg once or twice a day and increase to 400 mg if necessary.

2. Allopurinol*

Allopurinol is a more recent development and perhaps a more fundamental approach to the control of the uric acid body pool. The drug acts by inhibiting the enzyme xanthine oxidase which prevents the final step in the production of uric acid. This enzyme inhibition has been found quite useful in the management of urate supersaturation in the body, especially in those individuals with extreme hyperuricemia and secondary gout resulting from blood dyscrasias. In blocking the conversion of the xanthines to urates, the physician has a more direct control of urate levels without burdening the kidney with the excretion and reabsorption of huge amounts of this metabolite.

*Publisher's Note: Please refer to prescribing information available from the manufacturer for a complete presentation of contraindications, warnings, precautions, adverse reactions, and dosage.

An early question in allopurinol therapy was: "Would saturation of the system with xanthine and hypoxanthine create new problems and a new type of disease?" The answer to this in our practice so far has been negative. The xanthines in this form are highly soluble and readily excreted. Some experts theorize that xanthines act as a feedback mechanism in the purine cycle to slow down production.

a. Limitations

We have found that complications with allopurinol are few and infrequent. For the most part, they are quite benign and disappear when the drug is stopped. The principal side effect is gastric irritation or other gastrointestinal distress; however, dermatitis, ranging from mild to severe, has been reported.

We use dermatitis as a signal for immediate discontinuance of the drug. Much more rarely, there have been reports of serious side effects such as systemic toxicity with fever, blood dyscrasias, and possible hepatoxicity.

Some clinicians have suggested that allopurinol be restricted to the more severe cases of gout, especially those with gouty nephropathy, those whose gout has not responded to treatment with conventional uricosuric drugs, or those intolerant to probenecid or sulfinpyrazone. Our 12 years of experience with the drug indicates that it is relatively safe and effective.

In some new cases of gout, we have employed both probenecid and allopurinol during the early phase of treatment. After normal uric acid levels are achieved, however, we maintain the state with allopurinol alone.

b. Dosage

Allopurinol is usually started at 300 mg per day, and in many cases this is sufficient to produce the desired effect. In some patients, we have found it necessary to give 600 mg a day. The maximum daily dose is 800 mg.

Some practitioners tend to prescribe the drug in divided doses, but since the clinical half-life is quite long, we feel it is not really necessary. However, the use of divided doses may help avoid gastric distress.

3. Colchicine*

Colchicine is not a uricosuric agent and it does not reduce the plasma level or total body pool of urates. Nevertheless, it is such an integral part of therapy to control urate pathology that some mention should be made of its

---

*Publisher's Note: Please refer to prescribing information available from the manufacturer for a complete presentation of contraindications, warnings, precautions, adverse reactions, and dosage.

role. Colchicine apparently has some specific blocking action on chemotaxis in the acute gouty inflammatory process, possibly in blocking leukocyte response and lactic acid production.

It is believed that rapid change in body urate metabolism, especially the blood urate levels, somehow stimulates mechanisms leading to acute attacks of gouty arthritis. For this reason, it is often worthwhile to have the patient on prophylactic doses of colchicine to help prevent acute attacks that commonly occur when uricosuric therapy or allopurinol therapy is initiated.

It is our practice to prescribe prophylactic doses of colchicine during the first 6 months of therapy with uricosuric drugs or with allopurinol. A dose of 0.5 mg two or three times a day usually is quite adequate to achieve this prophylaxis.

We also use colchicine in prophylactic doses for gouty patients undergoing surgery. We begin a few days before surgery and continue for a week after. The same approach is useful for any other severe general stress in the gouty patient. Although we do not condone alcoholic or eating debauches for gout patients, if such is inevitable, we suggest they take the prophylactic doses of colchicine for several days or a week. Some clinicians recommend that colchicine be taken in prophylactic doses of 0.5 mg two to three times a day for an indefinite period.

In the treatment of acute gout, some clinicians recommend colchicine as the drug of first choice, giving 0.5 mg every hour until the patient gets relief or until diarrhea ensues.

We have found that in many patients, diarrhea is the first to make its appearance and is often accompanied by severe nausea and vomiting. In such high doses, colchicine is not a pleasant drug to take, and the patient can be served just as well with short-term high-dose therapy with phenylbutazone or indomethacin.

Some clinicians might consider giving colchicine, 1 mg IV, which can result in a striking benefit within a short time. Great care must be taken to avoid getting the colchicine outside the vein because of tissue necrosis. It is also possible that the drug may cause irritation of the endothelial lining of the vein wall itself. For dramatic effect, the clinician can consider an IM injection of corticotropin gel, 80 units.

H. Antibiotics*

Guidelines for diagnosing septic arthritis are presented in Chapter 2 and special tests and techniques are presented in Chapter 3. This section will provide some insights on the use of antibiotics.

Because of the wide variety of antibiotics available for specific problem areas, and the need for carefully calculated dosage, information presented in this segment of the chapter varies from the preceding segments. The information that follows represents examples of antibiotic use in selected arthritic conditions. The practitioner should consult the prescribing information available from the manufacturer for a complete presentation of individual products.

Direct instillation of most antibiotics into joint spaces should be avoided. One reason is that most commonly used antibiotics produce bactericidal levels in synovial fluid following parenteral administration. The not infrequent production of "chemical synovitis" is another reason to avoid direct instillation.

The gram stain is important in the initial treatment of septic arthritis, even before the culture results are known. If gram-positive cocci are seen, we select a synthetic penicillin derivative that is not affected by penicillinase. Nafcillin is preferred by many physicians because of greater in vitro activity against both penicillinase-producing staphylococci and penicillin-G-sensitive organisms. We employ an IV dose of 25 mg/Kg every six hours. Cephalosporins may be used, but if a penicillin allergy exists we administer erythromycin IV at 7.5 mg/Kg every six hours. If the culture eventually grows staphylococcus aureus and is penicillin resistant, nafcillin or other synthetic penicillins can be used. Dicloxacillin can be given orally at 10 to 15 mg/Kg every six hours.

Penicillin-G is still the preferred drug for sensitive staphylococci, pneumococci, and streptococci. With the former, we administer 50,000 to 70,000 U/Kg every six hours IV; in the latter two, 25,000 to 50,000 U/Kg.

We feel that parenteral antibiotics should be continued for two weeks. Appropriate oral antibiotics should be given for an additional four to six weeks when staphylococcal infections are involved.

Gram-negative cocci on stained smears should raise suspicion of gonococcus, particularly in the adult. A positive culture of gonococcus from a

---

*Publisher's Note: Please refer to prescribing information available from the manufacturer for a complete presentation of contraindications, warnings, precautions, adverse reactions, and dosage.

joint fluid or synovial tissue is definitive proof. However, the presence of gonococcus in the genital tract alone is not diagnostic and assumes the same role as Group A streptococcus in the pharynx of a patient with rheumatic fever. In our practice, treatment in those patients with gram-negative cocci is with penicillin-G at 50,000 to 70,000 U/Kg IV every six hours. If gonococcus is recovered on culture, the same program is continued for 10 to 14 days and oral penicillin is continued in many cases for an additional two weeks. Tetracycline and cephaloridine are alternatives. In the child, gram-negative cocci often mean hemophilus, and we give ampicillin IM 50 mg/Kg every six hours. If hemophilus is cultured, we continue treatment for two weeks. Hemophilus is also responsive to chloramphenicol and tetracycline.

The finding of gram-negative bacilli presents special problems. These patients often have underlying malignancies or are immunosuppressed, and two drugs may be required in critically ill patients with septicemia. We prefer cephaloridine in doses of 15 to 20 mg/Kg IM every 12 hours, kanamycin 7.5 mg/Kg IM every 12 hours, and polymyxin at 1.25 mg/Kg IM or IV, perhaps in that order. In these cases, intra-articular instillation of 5 to 10 mg of kanamycin or polymyxin may be required. Continued therapy with the appropriate antibiotic is contingent upon the culture and sensitivity reports. Pseudomonas, of course, require either gentamicin or carbenicillin, or both. If the smear is negative, we find it best to treat as if these were gram-negative cocci. In all cases of septic arthritis caused by bacteria, we feel that parenteral antibiotic administration should be used until the acute synovitis has subsided.

Acute inflammatory synovial fluid findings that later tend toward normal provide reassurance that control of the infection is being achieved. Only then do we substitute oral antibiotics.

Fungal infections and tuberculosis, though now quite rare, do present special problems. We feel that amphotericin B is a drug of choice for coccidioidomycosis, histoplasmosis, blastomycosis, cryptococcosis, and sporotrichosis. We employ penicillin-G for actinomycosis, and sulfadiazine for nocardiosis. Prolonged treatment is often needed, occasionally accompanied by such measures as synovectomy and excisions of soft tissue.

Infection with tubercle bacilli can be difficult to prove, and synovial biopsy is probably the best single means of being certain. We prefer treatment with a combination of agents. A popular combination is INH, at 300 mg per day, and PAS, 12 g of the *acid* daily, given in three or four divided doses. Streptomycin at one gram twice weekly can be substituted for PAS. We have used all three simultaneously, particularly when orthopedic procedures are involved. We have found that ethionamide is a new effective substitute for PAS. We continue treatment for at least one year or until all evidence of disease activity has disappeared.

I wish to acknowledge with gratitude the assistance of my colleague, Dr. Marvin H. Thomas, in the preparation of the section on antibiotics.

GENERAL REFERENCES

1. *Hollander, J. L. and McCarty, D. J., Jr., eds.:* Arthritis and Allied Conditions, *8th edition, Philadelphia, Lea & Febiger, 1972.*

2. *Boyle, J. A. and Buchanan, W. W.:* Clinical Rheumatology, *Philadelphia, F. A. Davis Company, 1971.*

3. Physicians' Desk Reference, *28th edition, Oradell, N. J., Medical Economics Company, 1974.*

4. Twentieth Rheumatism Review, *New York, The Arthritis Foundation, April 1973.*

5. *Rothermich, N. O.: An updated look at antirheumatic drugs, Med. Clin. N. Amer.* 51:*1213, September 1967.*

CHAPTER 7

Special Techniques
and Problems
in Treating
Arthritic Disorders

Daniel J. McCarty, Jr., M.D., F.A.C.P.
Professor of Medicine and Head
Section of Arthritis and Metabolic Diseases
Department of Medicine
The University of Chicago
Pritzker School of Medicine
Chicago, Illinois

CHAPTER 7

Special Techniques and Problems in Treating Arthritic Disorders

Daniel J. McCarty, Jr., M.D., F.A.C.P.

The purpose of this chapter is to present some special techniques used in managing various types of arthritis, and to discuss some approaches to certain related nonarticular complications that may occur.

A. Intrasynovial Adrenocorticosteroid Therapy

Since Hollander and his co-workers described the use of local injections of corticosteroids in 1951,[1] the effectiveness of this technique has been improved greatly by the development of microcrystalline suspensions of the less soluble esters.

The therapeutic goals for intrasynovial corticosteroid injection are summarized below:
- to help correct deformities accompanying inflammation in peripheral joints or tendons
- to help control inflammation in one or more particularly troublesome joints
- to provide optimal means of controlling a monarticular or oligoarticular arthritis
- to provide "medical synovectomy"
- to provide definitive treatment for isolated sterile inflammatory conditions such as:

  acute, nonspecific tenosynovitis
  acute and subacute bursitis

McCarty

It is important to realize that intrasynovial corticosteroid injection is considered an adjunctive form of treatment and is rarely the only means of treating a given condition.

The selection of a particular product should be based on the natural history of the condition being treated, the local pathologic changes, and the therapeutic goals. Since corticosteroids are basically anti-inflammatory drugs, they should not be used to treat lesions that are not inflammatory. Like all drugs, injectable steroids constitute a two-edged sword. Their use assumes a knowledge of the relevant anatomy and a reasonable degree of skill in arthrocentesis of various joints, tendons, and bursae. Steroids not injected into a synovial space will not do the job intended by the physician. (See the following table.)

Generic Name	Approximate Duration of Effect in Rheumatoid Arthritis	Usual Dose* Knee Joint	Finger Joint
Hydrocortisone acetate	6 days	25-50 mg	5-10 mg
Hydrocortisone tertiary butylacetate	12 days	25-50 mg	5-10 mg
Prednisolone tertiary butylacetate	14 days	20-40 mg	5 mg
Triamcinolone hexacetonide	28 days	20-40 mg	5 mg

*Other joints require intermediate doses.

NOTE: The above table was adapted from *Hollander, J. L.: Intrasynovial corticosteroid therapy. In* Arthritis and Allied Conditions, *ed. J. L. Hollander and D. J. McCarty, Jr., 8th edition, Philadelphia, Lea & Febiger, 1972, pp. 517-534.*

TABLE 1
Therapeutic Characteristics of Selected Corticosteroids

1. Arthrocentesis

Most peripheral joints can be entered with a needle, but this is more easily done in some joints than in others. The object is to puncture the synovial sac. Arthrocentesis is more easily performed in a joint that contains a large amount of fluid or one in which synovial proliferation has taken place.

With the exception of the hip and shoulder, joints are most readily entered from their extensor surfaces, because a swollen joint usually distends more in that direction, and the major nerves, arteries, and veins are generally found on the flexor surface of joints. Vital structures, such as major blood vessels and nerves, should not be traumatized. Thorough knowledge of anatomy is essential. Moreover, knowledge of the disease process and how it might alter normal relationships is invaluable. A careful examination of the affected joint and inspection of adequate roentgenograms should precede any joint entry with a needle.

It is important to minimize pain. Articular cartilage has no intrinsic pain fibers. Synovial membrane has only those which accompany its nutrient vessels, but the articular capsule and the periosteum of the neighboring bony structures are richly supplied with nerves. If the joint is large and contains a large effusion, no anesthesia may be required. Ethyl chloride, sprayed briefly on the skin overlying the potential puncture site, often is sufficient.

If the joint is small, the patient tense, or the physician inexperienced, local anesthetic injection should precede arthrocentesis. After a small wheal is made in the skin by injecting about 0.5 ml of procaine hydrochloride with a 25-gauge needle, the joint capsule is infiltrated and the adjacent periosteum is "stippled" by light applications of the small needle. The joint space is then entered, using a 20-gauge needle. Occasionally, as when numerous rice bodies are present, a larger bore needle is required. Injection of corticosteroids into small joints is carried out with a small 25-gauge needle.

It is important to avoid infection. Disposable syringes and needles are routinely employed. The skin is prepared with iodine and alcohol, as for any other procedure of this type. We have found that drapes, sterile gloves, and surgical masks are not necessary.

a. Limitations and precautions

Arthrocentesis should not be considered in the presence of the following:
- bacterial or fungal infection in joint, periarticular structure, or overlying skin
- lateral instability of a weight-bearing joint due to capsular or ligamentous laxity, or to cartilaginous or bony destruction.

Practical limitations to arthrocentesis include:
- injection not technically feasible for anatomical reasons
- prior failure to control inflammation for a reasonable period of time after technically satisfactory injection.

Local infection of the skin or other periarticular structures is an obvious deterrent to the procedure. Equally dangerous is the existence of concomitant bacteremia. It is impossible to insert a needle through an inflamed synovium without trauma to at least a few capillaries. Organisms may be inoculated into the joint from infected blood. Therefore, not all joint infections after arthrocentesis are caused by faulty aseptic technique.

Clinical and experimental evidence indicates that too frequently repeated injections of corticosteroids into a joint may be injurious to the articular cartilage. Initially there may be acute inflammatory reactions to the crystals. Cartilage destruction may occur later. This damage has been ascribed to relief of pain encouraging overuse of the diseased joint. Of course, no more than minimally effective doses of steroid should be injected, and they should be made at intervals as long as possible.

b. Injection techniques for specific joints
Knee
The knee is entered from the medial surface so that the needle enters the space between the patella and the patellar groove of the femur. The knee is kept fully extended. The patient must not contract the quadriceps muscle as this will clamp the patella firmly in its groove and thwart any attempt to advance the needle tip. Even in the case of a small effusion, it is rarely necessary to advance the needle to the hub; frequently, one-half inch of penetration is sufficient. It is important to avoid damaging the articular cartilage with the needle. This procedure may be painful if the periosteum is struck with the needle tip.

If there is a large amount of fluid present, it is preferable to enter the suprapatellar bursae just lateral and superior to the patella. At this site puncture is almost painless.

Ankle
The ankle joint is readily entered with a leg-foot angle of 90°. The needle is inserted vertically at a point just medial to the extensor hallucis tendon on a line with the medial malleolus.

Subtalar joint
The subtalar joint is readily entered with the leg-foot angle kept at 90°. Here the needle is directed horizontally on a line with the tip of the external malleolus at a point just proximal to the sinus tarsi.

Tarsal joints and tarsometatarsal joints
These joints can rarely be entered.

Metatarsophalangeal joints
These joints are relatively easy to inject from their extensor surfaces. The space between the metatarsal head and the base of the first phalanx is first identified by marking the overlying skin with fingernail pressure. The skin is then prepared in the usual manner. After appropriate local anesthesia, a

20-gauge needle may be inserted vertically into the joint. Traction on the corresponding toe is often helpful.

Toe joints

These very tiny joints require use of a 25-gauge needle. It has not been our practice to inject toe joints unless they are unusually troublesome.

Hip

Arthrocentesis of this joint is analogous to a spinal tap. It is an essentially blind procedure, and close attention must be paid to appropriate anatomical landmarks. A 20-gauge needle two-and-a-half inches long is inserted into the skin from the anterior direction at the point of intersection of a vertical line from the anterior superior spine of the ilium and a horizontal line from the greater trochanter. The femoral artery is generally two finger-breadths medial to this point. The hip is kept in internal rotation during the procedure. The needle is directed posteromedially, and the shaft of the needle should make an angle of approximately 60° with the frontal plane. The tip of the needle is gently advanced until firm resistance is met (articular cartilage) and then withdrawn slightly as gentle suction is employed. Unless fluid is obtained, the results of corticosteroid injection are unpredictable and often unsatisfactory.

Shoulder

The shoulder joint may be easily entered from its anterior surface by directing the needle just below the tip of the coracoid process and just medial to the head of the humerus, or from a posterior approach just beneath the acromion. Effusion of the shoulder is usually found anterolaterally.

Acromioclavicular joint

This joint is frequently involved in rheumatoid arthritis and is often a cause of shoulder pain when the patient is recumbent. It can easily be identified by palpation along the clavicle until a defect is felt. A 23-gauge needle is inserted vertically from above, directly into the joint space after appropriate use of local anesthesia.

Sternoclavicular joint

This is best entered from a point directly anterior to the joint. The tip of the needle is inserted between the inferior border of the clavicle and the first rib so that the latter remains as a shield between the needle tip and the lung, avoiding pneumothorax. We have injected this joint only rarely because aspiration is not easily accomplished.

Elbow

The joint margin may be readily identified on the extensor surface lateral to the olecranon process with the joint at 90°. The needle is inserted just lateral to the olecranon and just below the lateral epicondyle of the humerus so that the needle is parallel to the shaft of the radius. The radiohumeral articulation can also be entered by first identifying the joint margin and then inserting the needle perpendicular to the skin. Since these two joint spaces communicate, it is usually possible to inject or aspirate both with one puncture.

Wrist

The wrist joint proper can be easily entered dorsally after identification of the joint line which lies between the radial and ulnar styloid processes. Local anesthetic injection, with insertion of a small bore needle into the joint, aids in gauging the proper plane that should be employed. Generally, the wrist is entered at a point just distal to the radius approximately two fingerbreadths ulnar to the anatomic snuffbox. The bursa underlying the fibrocartilaginous articular disk of the distal radioulnar joint often communicates with the distal radioulnar joint and is often the site of rheumatoid inflammation. This sac can be punctured from the extensor surface at a point just distal to the ulnar bone.

Small hand joints

These joints are best entered from the extensor surface from either side. A distended or hypertrophic synovium almost always bulges dorsally, and it is relatively easy to place a needle under the extensor tendon. Fluid is rarely obtained. The material to be injected will distend the joint so that one can feel and see the joint bulge on all sides. If this has been accomplished, the joint space has been entered. The metacarpophalangeal joints may be entered in similar fashion, or, if distention is minimal, the joint line may be identified with the joint at 90° of flexion before inserting the needle.

Temporomandibular joint

This joint may be entered rather easily just below the zygomatic arch at a point one fingerbreadth in front of the ear. Entry is often facilitated if the patient is instructed to open his mouth wide.[2]

2. Correction of Deformities

The range of motion of joints affected with rheumatoid arthritis, psoriatic arthritis, etc., may be limited as the flexor muscles contract and the extensors atrophy. Such deformity may occur rapidly (a few days or weeks), most notably in knee and elbow joints. As these joints can be injected easily, local steroid therapy can readily be given. After 24 to 48 hours, as inflammation subsides, physical therapy in the form of hot or cold applications and range of motion exercises can be confidently expected to correct the deformity, with complete or nearly complete recovery of lost function (see Chapter 5). The sooner flexion deformity is treated, the better the result. Other synovial structures amenable to such treatment include the flexor tendons of the fingers, the proximal interphalangeal and metacarpophalangeal joints, wrists, and shoulders.

If these measures do not correct the deformity, a consultation with a specialist in arthritis management should be obtained. If the natural history of the disease is one of sustained inflammation with progressive deformity, as in rheumatoid arthritis, a very long-acting corticosteroid can be chosen to achieve a "medical synovectomy," as described below.

3. "Medical Synovectomy"

Histologic examination of rheumatoid synovium shows infiltration of mononucleated inflammatory cells, sometimes to the point that the appearance of the tissue resembles a lymph node. These cells are not present in normal synovium and are engaged in immunoglobulin synthesis. These are secreted into the extracellular fluid and are phagocytosed by polymorphonuclear leukocytes, resulting in lysosomal enzyme release and cumulative joint damage. This damage is perceived clinically as progressive anatomical and functional deterioration.[3] (The reader is referred to Reference 3 for a more complete discussion of pathogenesis.) Evidence of tissue healing exists side by side with chronic inflammation—e.g., fibroblastic proliferation and phagocytosis of debris by tissue macrophages. The aim of "medical synovectomy" by injection of potent long-acting steroids is to permit healing to progress unhampered by continuous inflammation.

Clinical evidence suggests that joint motion aggravates inflammation; conversely, resting a joint by splints has been shown by Gault and Spyker to be anti-inflammatory.[4] The potentiating effect of joint motion has been shown experimentally in crystal-induced inflammation in canine joints by Agudelo, Schumacher, and Phelps.[5] It is our practice to rest a joint for a prolonged period of time after injecting long-acting steroids.[6] In addition to preventing additional inflammation, this practice spares the cartilage from possible harmful effects of the drug. It is important to take a splinted joint out of its splint and put it through a full range of motion daily. This avoids contractures caused by fibrosis of joint capsules and ligaments and by the shortening of tendons spanning the joint.

We typically protect a knee or other weight-bearing joint for six to eight weeks after the injection of triamcinolone hexacetonide, using bed rest or crutch walking or both. We use slings for shoulders or elbow joints and splints for wrists, carpal, and small hand joints for at least three weeks after injection. In one study, 88 percent of injected synovial structures in rheumatoid patients remained uninflamed 22 months later.[6] As with surgical synovectomy, late recurrences are common, although nearly 25 percent of these structures were in full local remission five years later. The ability of this compound to produce tissue atrophy is great. For this reason, it should not be injected other than intra-articularly. Even the drug leaking out of the joint along the needle track has produced cosmetically undesirable effects in the skin and subcutaneous tissue. Because of these complications, the decision to use either medical or surgical therapy to control inflammation is best made in consultation with a qualified rheumatologist.

4. Monarticular Arthritis, Bursitis, and Nonspecific Tenosynovitis

There are numerous times in clinical practice when one is faced with tenosynovitis (see Chapter 2) or bursitis: e.g., supraspinatus (subacromial), olecranon (trochanteric), anserine, calcaneal; or periarthritis, e.g., adhesive capsulitis of the shoulder. Local corticosteroids can reverse the disease process quickly and efficiently, and I have seen remissions far exceeding a reasonable estimate of local steroid persistence. A medium- or short-acting steroid can be chosen. Here a common practice is to dilute the steroid crystal suspension to the desired volume with one percent procaine hydrochloride. This provides immediate useful information to the physician. For if pain is immediately relieved, it is likely that the injection will prove effective. This is particularly true in treating a partially frozen shoulder caused by adhesive capsulitis. In my practice, I prepare a mixture of 50 ml of normal saline, 10 ml of procaine hydrochloride, and 20 to 40 mg of prednisolone tertiary butylacetate which is injected directly into the shoulder joint, greatly distending it. To take advantage of the presence of the medication, physical therapy is begun 48 hours later. Unless the physician possesses unusual skill in arthrocentesis, it is advisable to seek the help of a specialist for this form of therapy.

An adequate knowledge of the anatomy of the involved parts is most important when corticosteroids are injected for local conditions such as bursitis and tenosynovitis. Reference to an anatomical atlas or model is usually necessary, unless the technique is frequently practiced.

Injection of prednisolone tertiary butylacetate in an amount proportional to the size of the inflamed bursa or tendon sheath is also necessary. The subacromial (subdeltoid) bursa at the shoulder is relatively easily penetrated by inserting a 22-gauge needle lateral to, and slightly anterior to, the acromion of the scapula. The needle is inserted horizontally to a depth of about 3 cm into the tender bursa, and the steroid is injected. Further anteriorly and slightly below the head of the humerus is the site of injection for tendinitis of the long head of the biceps muscle. The needle is pointed slightly upward into the bicipital groove, injecting the steroid.

Tennis elbow is treated locally by injecting the steroid into the point of tenderness just lateral to the capitellum of the lateral epicondyle of the humerus, and distally near the head of the radius. A penetration of about 1 cm of a 25-gauge needle will reach the bursa or inflamed muscle area. Olecranon bursitis is easily injected from the medial or lateral side at the point of the elbow into the sac.

Carpal tunnel syndrome* can be ameliorated by injection of steroid into the common flexor tendon sheath on the volar side of the wrist. The needle is inserted with the patient's fist clenched. The 25-gauge needle is inserted proximal to the pisiform bone, just lateral to the flexor palmaris tendon, pointed slightly distally, to a depth of about 1 cm. The patient then opens his fist, insuring that no tendon has been pierced, and the steroid should be injected without undue pressure on the plunger of the syringe. Ganglia of the wrist are aspirated and injected easily over the fluctuant or distended sac. Tenosynovitis at the radial styloid (DeQuervain's disease*) responds promptly to steroid injected from a site just distal to the radial styloid over the conjoined tendon on the radial side of the thumb. Trigger finger* and snapping thumb are injected using a 25-gauge needle. These tendon sheaths are penetrated just distal to the metacarpophalangeal joint, usually at a depth of 5 mm. If the needle is within the tendon sheath, gentle active movement of the involved finger by the patient can be felt as a crepitation through the needle and syringe, and the steroid should be injected gently.

Trochanteric bursitis responds well to corticosteroid injection. The maximal point of tenderness on palpation is behind and slightly above the prominence of the trochanter. The 22-gauge needle is inserted horizontally and medially to a depth of 3 to 4 cm, usually producing sharp local pain as the bursa is reached. Prepatellar bursitis is injected, after aspiration, from a medial or lateral direction just anterior to and distal to the lower margin of the patella. Anserine bursitis occurs just below the knee, anterior to the medial plateau of the tibia. Local injection of steroid is made with a 25-gauge needle.

Tendinitis* or tenosynovitis at the ankle or instep is injected similarly to such conditions at the wrist, as described above.

Calcaneal bursitis is injected from the medial or lateral side of the heel, using a 23-gauge needle. Bunions should be aspirated and injected from the dorsal side, not from the medial or plantar aspects. Injection of steroid through a 25-gauge needle is recommended.

5. Complications of Intrasynovial Steroid Therapy
As previously mentioned, steroids are injected as microcrystalline suspensions. The crystal size is similar to the sodium urate crystals in gout and the calcium pyrophosphate crystals in pseudogout. Therefore, it is not surprising that about two percent of steroid injections cause a transient inflamma-

---

*Publisher's note: Based on a review of corticosteroids by the National Academy of Sciences—National Research Council and/or other information, the Food and Drug Administration has classified this indication as possibly effective at this time. See the prescribing information for specific products.

tion ("postinjection flare"). Such inflammation has been induced in normal human and canine joints.[7] The patient should be forewarned of this possibility at the time of injection. Applications of ice packs and simple analgesics will usually alleviate the symptoms, which invariably subside completely in 24 to 48 hours, as the anti-inflammatory action of the steroid predominates. It is probably best to minimize use of the joint for at least several days after local injection.

If symptoms of inflammation persist beyond this time or if they recur acutely during the next week, after a temporary improvement, infection should be suspected and arthrocentesis again undertaken with a white cell count and culture of joint fluid. Infection is exceedingly rare if sterile precautions have been taken and the limitations to injection listed on page 133 have been considered.

The most serious complication of intrasynovial steroid treatment is metabolic damage to joint cartilage and underlying bone. Profound suppression of chondrocyte protein synthesis by steroid has been described in rabbit joints,[8] as has marked joint deterioration.[9] This is another reason to rest the joint after injection, especially if long-acting esters like triamcinolone hexacetonide are used. Rapid devolutionary joint changes have been described in humans as well as in rabbits.[10,11] This potential damage has not often been noted in human joints unless excessive doses of steroids have been used repeatedly or unless the joints were abused after injection.

B. Nonarticular Manifestations of Arthritis

1. Gouty nephropathy

Deposition of monosodium urate crystals in the interstitial renal tissue may compromise renal function in gouty patients. It has never been established conclusively that treatment can result in reversal of these lesions, but it is reasonable to expect that proper treatment can result in preservation of residual renal function. The treatment of choice in this situation is allopurinol in dosages sufficient to keep the body fluids undersaturated with respect to uric acid, preventing further urate crystals from forming (usually 200 to 800 mg daily in divided doses) (see Chapter 6).

2. Uric acid stones and gravel

Uric acid, not sodium urate, may precipitate in the urine in variable quantity. Classically, such gravel or stones have a pink appearance, looking like brick dust. Large quantities may block urine flow completely. Urologic intervention with cystoscopy and irrigation with alkaline buffers through uretheral catheters reopens the urinary system. This complication is often preventable by maintenance of good urine flow rate, alkalization of the urine to pH 6 or greater by prescribing sodium or potassium salts of weak acids, such as sodium bicarbonate. If the patient shows a marked tendency to form stones, particularly if he is an overexcretor of uric acid (>600 mg uric acid per 24 hours on a low-purine diet), allopurinol should be prescribed.

3. Rheumatoid vasculitis

A dreaded and often fatal manifestation of rheumatoid arthritis is a syndrome including one or more of the following: peripheral neuropathy, cutaneous ulcers or areas of gangrene, pleuritis, pericarditis, and scleritis. Such patients should be managed primarily by a consultant rheumatologist. No controlled data are available, but it is presently believed that the lives of many of these patients can be salvaged.

4. Rheumatoid lung disease

Interstitial fibrosis, rheumatoid pleuritis, and rheumatoid nodules may occur in the lung. The latter may cavitate, simulating an abscess, or may perforate into the pleural space giving rise to a bronchopleural fistula or to pneumothorax. These latter complications are treated by water seal drainage or with surgery.

5. Rheumatoid pericarditis

This relatively rare complication may result in asymptomatic friction rubs, cardiac tamponade, or constrictive pericarditis. Mild tamponade may respond to aspiration of pericardial fluids and systemic corticosteroid, but many cases will require pericardectomy. Constrictive pericarditis should always be treated surgically. The rheumatoid process may also affect the valves and myocardium.

6. Joint rupture

Regardless of etiology, any knee joint with a relatively recent effusion may rupture because of the extremely high intra-articular pressure resulting when such a joint is flexed. The fluid contents of the knee leaks out at the site of rupture (which is usually posteriorly in the area of the popliteal fossa) into the calf. The result resembles thrombophlebitis, with pitting edema, local tenderness, and a positive Homan's sign. The absence of a palpable cord representing a thrombosed vein and a history of a recently swollen joint no longer detectable on physical examination suggest the diagnosis. Confirmation is effected easily by an arthrogram with demonstration of the posterior joint rupture. I have found that treatment of the synovitis with rest and intra-articular corticosteroids is uniformly satisfactory.

REFERENCES

1. Hollander, J. L., Brown, E. M., Jr., Jessar, R. A., and Brown, C. Y.: Hydrocortisone and cortisone injected into arthritic joints: comparative effects of and use of hydrocortisone as a local antiarthritic agent, JAMA 147:1629, December 22, 1951.

2. Hollander, J. L.: Intrasynovial corticosteroid therapy. In Arthritis and Allied Conditions, *ed. J. L. Hollander and D. J. McCarty, Jr., 8th edition, Philadelphia, Lea & Febiger, 1972, pp. 517-534.*

3. Zvaifler, N. J.: Pathogenetic mechanisms in rheumatoid arthritis. In Arthritis and Allied Conditions, *ed. J. L. Hollander and D. J. McCarty, Jr., 8th edition, Philadelphia, Lea & Febiger, 1972, pp. 302-308.*

4. Gault, S. J. and Spyker, J. M.: Beneficial effect of immobilization of joints in rheumatoid and related arthritides: a splint study using sequential analysis, Arthritis Rheum. 12:34, February 1969.

5. Agudelo, C. A., Schumacher, H. R., and Phelps, P.: Effect of exercise on urate crystal-induced inflammation in canine joints, Arthritis Rheum. 15:609, November-December 1972.

6. McCarty, D. J.: Treatment of rheumatoid joint inflammation with triamcinolone hexacetonide, Arthritis Rheum. 15:157, March-April 1972.

7. McCarty, D. J., Jr. and Hogan, J. M.: Inflammatory reaction after intrasynovial injection of microcrystalline adrenocorticosteroid esters, Arthritis Rheum. 7:359, August 1964.

8. Mankin, H. J. and Conger, K. A.: The acute effects of intra-articular hydrocortisone on articular cartilage in rabbits, J. Bone Joint Surg. 48-A:1383, October 1966.

9. Salter, R. B., Gross, A., and Hall, J. H.: Hydrocortisone arthropathy—an experimental investigation, Canad. Med. Ass. J. 97:374, August 19, 1967.

10. Chandler, G. N., Wright, V., and Hartfall, S. J.: Intra-articular therapy in rheumatoid arthritis: comparison of hydrocortisone tertiary butyl acetate and hydrocortisone acetate, Lancet 2:659, September 1958.

11. Chandler, G. N. and Wright, V.: Deleterious effect of intra-articular hydrocortisone, Lancet 2:661, September 1958.

CHAPTER 8

An Overview
of Surgical Procedures
in Arthritis

Lee Ramsay Straub, M.D., F.A.C.S.

Professor of Clinical Surgery
Cornell University Medical College
New York, New York

Attending Orthopaedic Surgeon
Hospital for Special Surgery
New York Hospital

Consultant
Bronx Veterans Administration Hospital

CHAPTER 8

An Overview
of Surgical Procedures
in Arthritis

Lee Ramsay Straub, M.D., F.A.C.S.

A. Introduction

Surgery in the arthritic patient has two purposes: relief of pain and correction of deformity, both of which can help to restore function. Certain procedures, such as synovectomy and joint realignment by osteotomy, may have a beneficial or even prophylactic effect on the disease process. Correction of a congenital or rachitic bowleg in youth may well prevent disabling degenerative arthritis in later life. For the most part, however, surgery in arthritis is aimed at salvaging joints that are partially or completely destroyed by a disease process.

While there are great differences between osteoarthritis and rheumatoid arthritis, the surgical repair of an involved joint may be similar or identical in both diseases. In this chapter, common areas of involvement with accepted nonsurgical and surgical means of correction will be identified by disease.

B. Osteoarthritis

Osteoarthritis is a degenerative process of joints subsequent to congenital or traumatic misalignment or to infectious change. Found in weight-bearing joints and in areas of repeated stress, it is characterized by marginal

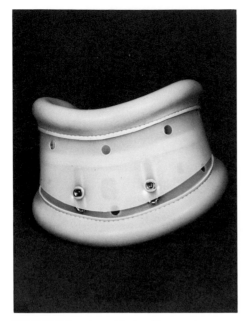 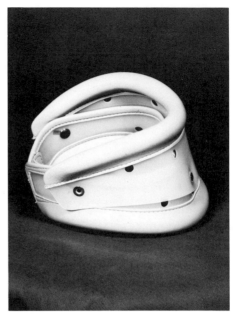

FIGURE 1a—A molded collar used for cervical support.

FIGURE 1b—Another view of the molded collar.

osteophytic production, subarticular cyst formation, loss of articular cartilage, and even osteonecrosis. Degenerative changes in the spine are frequently in the cervical or lower lumbar areas.

1. Spine

The neck, excessively mobile, inadequate to the weight of the head, traumatized by sports or automobile accidents, suffers disc disease and secondary arthritis to intervertebral and facet articulations. Nerve root radiculitis may appear. Most neck complaints are relieved by a supportive collar (Figures 1a, 1b), traction, rest, and guided exercise. However, persistent and extreme pain may require arthrodesis of involved cervical vertebrae, disc excision, and decompression of nerve roots.[1] In the past this was done from the back of the neck, but in recent years some very efficient anterior fusion techniques have been devised.[2]

The lumbar spine is the site of many congenital variants that may cause painful degenerative disease. Further, the lower lumbar joints are subject to heavy loading and trauma in work and play. The greatest frequency of disc degeneration and rupture occurs at the last lumbar and at the lumbosacral joints. Here again, in spite of even advanced x-ray changes, relief may be provided by rest, proper support, and especially postural exercises. If these measures are not sufficient, spinal fusion or disc excision or both may be required. The choice of treatment and the surgical approach is individualized.

2. Upper extremity

Osteoarthritis in the joints of the upper extremities is far less frequent than in the lower extremities. A peculiar, possibly familial variety produces

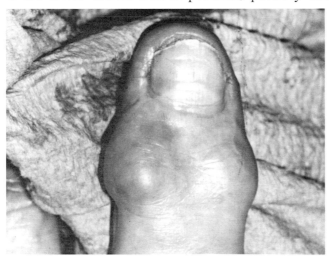

FIGURE 2
A view of Heberden's
nodes.

enlargement and deformity of the distal interphalangeal joints of the hands. Common in women of middle age, the pain and persistent joint swelling (Figure 2), (Heberden's node), usually subside spontaneously.[3,4] A mucous cyst arising on a node may be excised.[5] The underlying bony spur that originates from the interphalangeal joint margin must be removed.

Degenerative arthritis at the base of the thumb (trapezio-metacarpal joint) can be very disabling. In a joint that requires mobility with stability, painful arthritis may be the result of congenital variant or old injury (dislocation or Bennett's fracture). Rest provided with a carefully molded removable splint for three or four months often provides relief. If this fails, there are three operative choices: arthrodesis of the trapezio-metacarpal joint,[6] resection of the trapezium in its entirety,[7] or, more recently, substitution of the trapezium by a prosthesis. Good results have been obtained by the two former approaches; the latter remains uncertain, awaiting longer experience.

Wrist pain is detrimental to hand function. Degenerative changes at the wrist may follow fracture or ligament injury. Intracarpal dislocations are easily missed. They may eventuate in arthritis, and may encroach on the volar carpal tunnel to compress the median nerve.

The operative selection varies with the individual problem. For diffuse carpal changes, arthrodesis by one of many methods is the prime choice; for stability without pain it is preferable to painful mobility. For localized changes between proximal carpal bones and distal radius, proximal row carpectomy bears consideration on the basis of good long-term experience. Resection of the distal ulna (Darrach procedure)[8] may relieve a painful, post-traumatic distal radioulnar joint. Symptoms of medial nerve compression (the carpal tunnel syndrome) are overcome by division of the transverse carpal ligament.[9]

Various devices for carpal bone replacement and "total" wrist substitutions are in the developmental stage at this time. Their eventual use will be better directed to severe rheumatoid wrists rather than to the osteoarthritic wrist.

Reconstructive procedures at the elbow are more often needed by the patient with rheumatoid arthritis than with obsteoarthritis. Degenerative changes following severe injury may require carefully individualized procedures.

Osteoarthritis of the shoulder region is relatively uncommon. Again it follows trauma, tendon cuff degeneration, and, rarely, metabolic disease. Even less common is the need for surgery. Beyond shoulder cuff repair, most painful complaints are relieved by rest, heat, and guided exercise. For severe and lasting pain, the surgical choices are arthrodesis and replacement of the humeral head with a Neer prosthesis (Figure 3). Arthrodesis has provided satisfactory function and is the most certain way to provide shoulder comfort. Resection of the outer end of the clavicle at the acromioclavicular joint will reduce pain and increase shoulder motion when arthritic change has occurred.

3. Hip

Degenerative arthritis of the hip may be idiopathic or secondary to congenital variants, Calve-Legg-Perthes disease, trauma, or infection. Of greatest importance in arthritis prevention is early recognition of disease processes of the hip in childhood, for it is here that most of the idiopathic degenerative hips of middle age find their origin.

Weekly clinical neonatal hip rounds in a large obstetrical center have discovered a surprising number of dysplastic hips that, when corrected by a simple splint (Figure 4), will avoid future degenerative arthritis and surgery.[10]

A limp or pain in the hip or knee of a growing child or adolescent may be the first sign of Perthes disease or of a slipping of the femoral capital epiphysis. Early recognition and treatment by rest or a splint for the former and surgical fixation for the latter are essential to normal function in adult life.

150

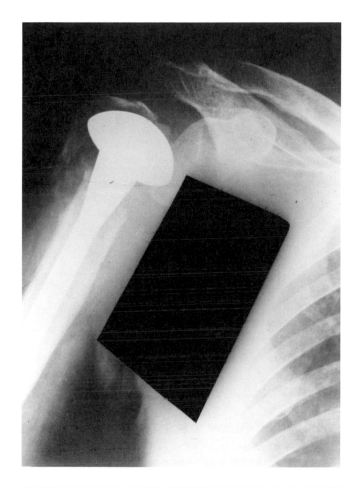

FIGURE 3
The Neer prosthesis
that replaces the head
of the humerus.

FIGURE 4
A malleable splint that
provides hip abduction
for dysplasia or
dislocation.

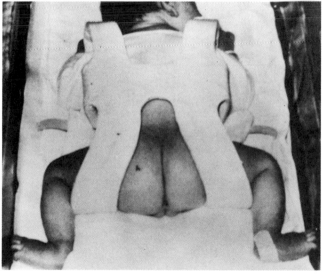

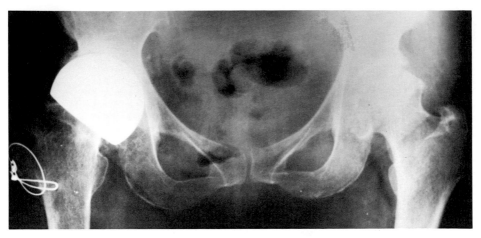

FIGURE 5—A cup arthroplasty for degenerative arthritis of the hip.

Fortunately, septic arthritis of the newborn is now infrequent. At the hip it is recognized by fever, joint tenderness, and rigid splinting. It may be confirmed by aspiration of purulent material. Treatment with antibiotics is not enough. Immediate surgical drainage is imperative if the femoral head is to be preserved.

Any of these conditions, as well as trauma, may lead to hip arthritis, which is common and frequently disabling. Many operations to provide relief were devised at the beginning of the century. They included fusions, resection, various osteotomies, and arthroplasties using cartilage, or fascial or foreign membranes as interpositional material.

Smith-Petersen introduced the cup arthroplasty procedure in 1935.[11] A metal cup, highly polished, is placed between the socket of the acetabulum and the head of the femur (Figure 5). This provides a smooth bearing surface on both sides of the joint. The long-term results of the cup arthroplasty have generally been satisfactory. Some, in good hands and in properly selected patients, have been excellent. Shortly after the introduction of the cup for arthroplasty, prostheses that replaced the femoral head were devised. The first popular femoral head prosthesis was that of John and Robert Judet. These prostheses functioned well, but the acrylic material was not well tolerated. A myriad of devices soon followed—usually of metal—consisting of a ball to replace the femoral head and a stem implanted in the femoral neck or shaft. They were not cemented into the bone.

Unfortunately, these devices, cups, and prostheses did not always provide relief of pain. Some penetrated and some stems loosened, requiring removal.

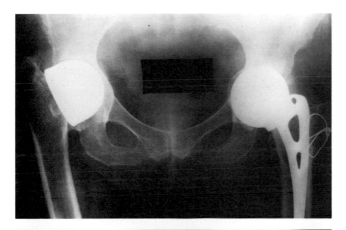

FIGURE 6a
A Moore prosthesis that replaces the left femoral head and neck. A Smith-Peterson cup is on the right.

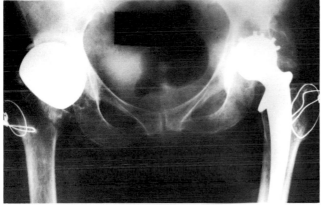

FIGURE 6b
A metal to metal McKee—Farrar prosthesis that replaces the left hip. The spikes on the acetabular component are set in "cement," as is the femoral stem.

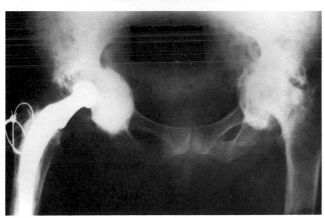

FIGURE 6c
The Charnley type of "total hip." The wires at the side of the femoral stem immobilize the greater trochanter, which was removed to facilitate the surgical exposure. The position of the radio-transplant plastic cup is indicated by the wire imbedded in it. The "cement" used here is radio-opaque.

The chief credit for bringing hip replacement to its present level belongs to John Charnley of England.[12] He and his co-workers have spent many years in study of materials and designs for artificial hips. Many other individuals and centers have become involved, and more than a score of "total hips" have been introduced. Basically they consist of a cup to replace the acetabular socket and a ball on a stem to replace the femoral head and neck (Figures 6a, 6b, 6c). While in some devices both ball and socket are metal,

153

most use a high-density plastic for the acetabular cup and metal for the femoral component. These parts are fixed to the pelvis and femoral shaft by a plastic cement, methymethacrylate. This putty-like material becomes rock-hard in eight to ten minutes after preparation, thus holding each part of the prosthesis in place in the prepared bone.

While the "total hip" operation is indicated for the severely degenerated hip and results are generally outstanding, it does "burn the bridge" in that much acetabular and all of the femoral head and neck are removed. Should there be serious complication, infection, or loosening, requiring removal of the device, salvage procedures are less than satisfactory. Thus there remains a place for osteotomy, which, by realignment and possibly by cir-culatory alteration, may relieve pain and even restore articular space in x-ray. There is also a place for cup arthroplasty, especially in younger patients, because far less tissue is removed and salvage, when necessary, can often be achieved.

4. Knee

Deformities due to rickets are far fewer now than a generation or two ago, but bowlegs still occur. Bowlegs and knock-knees can cause disabling osteoarthritis of the knees in later life. If these conditions persist in spite of medical management during early adolescence, surgical correction by osteotomy is indicated.[13,14] Correctional braces are cumbersome and inef-fective. If uncorrected in youth, congenital variants in knee anatomy caus-ing patellar instability or dislocation will eventually lead to osteoarthritis. In sports, prevention and recognition of internal derangements of the knee are increasingly important in our expanding athletic programs. Meniscal tears and ligamentous instability are frequent precursors of knee joint degeneration.

Knee pain is always accompanied by atrophy of both the quadriceps and hamstring musculature. Basic to all therapy for the painful arthritic knee is a supervised program of muscle-building exercises. They must be individ-ualized to the patient's needs and symptoms, but are often the only treat-ment required. Braces and knee cages have a limited use, especially during sports. Aspiration with or without steroid injections is useful for infrequent hydroarthrosis, but frequent steroid injection is to be discouraged as it may speed the degenerative process. Should there be varus or valgus deformity and reasonable articular space remains, as seen in a standing anterior-pos-terior x-ray of the knee, correction should be done by an appropriate osteotomy.

If there is extensive loss of articular cartilage in the medial or lateral joint compartment, but not in both, replacement of a single tibial plateau by

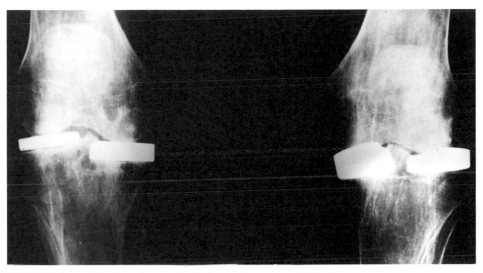

FIGURE 7a—A MacIntosh prosthesis that replaces the tibial plateau.

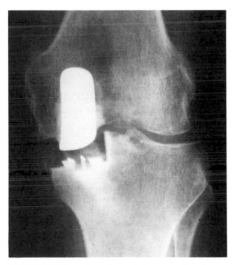

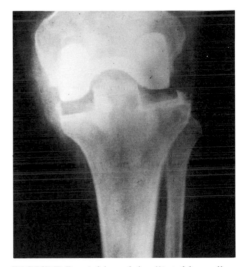

FIGURE 7b—A unicondylar prosthesis
that replaces the medial knee joint.
The tibial component is of high-density
polyester. Both components are
"cemented" in place.

FIGURE 7c—A bicondylar "total knee."

MacIntosh prosthesis can be done.[15] This device, available in graded
heights, can be used to correct moderate angular deformities (Figures 7a,
7b, 7c, 7d) at the knee, and provides a smooth articular substitute for both
tibial plateaus. Severe, painful intra-articular change, with or without an-
gulation, calls for knee joint replacement with bicondylar prosthesis, as
first devised by Gunston,[16] or by a hinge prosthesis.[17,18,19] The latter is more
often required when severe arthritic change is associated with marked angular deformity and instability, as in advanced rheumatoid disease.

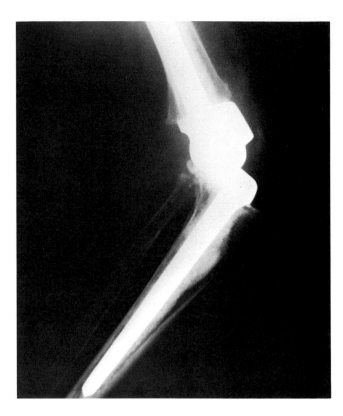

FIGURE 7d
A metal hinge that
replaces the knee joint.

A stiff knee may in itself be disabling. Arthrodesis is, therefore, reserved for the salvage or unsuccessful prosthetic arthroplasty, or for the treatment of resistant infection, especially tuberculosis.

5. Ankle and foot

Osteoarthritis of the ankle is unusual. The result of injury, its prevention rests in the recognition and thorough treatment of ligamentous tears, even by open surgery when indicated, and by precise reduction of fractures around or in the ankle joint. Ankle arthritis may also follow infection or past inflammatory arthritis.

Temporary relief of pain can be provided by immobilization in plaster cast or molded Hessing brace.[20,21] Since a stiff but painless ankle, in good position, may be very functional, arthrodesis is the definitive treatment.

Through congenital or traumatic misalignment the various tarsal joints may develop arthritic changes. Because of the demands of weight bearing, these changes are progressive and very painful. Judicious use of stiff arches made on a mold of the foot, as well as stiff-soled shoes to serve as splints, may provide relief. If these measures fail, selected joint fusions are required.

156

In like fashion, the great toe affected by osteoarthritis of the first metatarsophalangeal joint (hallus rigidus), with or without bunion deformity, may get complete relief of pain by use of a stiff shoe sole (a steel shank between the layers of leather) with a metatarsal rocker to provide the natural forward roll in take-off. There are a number of useful operations for the correction of painful bunions.[22] They include tendon transplants, realignment by osteotomy, osteoplasty of the metatarsal head, hemiphalangectomy, and arthrodesis.

C. Rheumatoid Arthritis

Much of what has been said above concerning the conservative and surgical care of the patient with osteoarthritis applies to the rheumatoid patient as well. However, the basic conditions are vastly different. Rheumatoid arthritis represents a bodily disease with multiple joint involvement characterized by expansion of disease synovium. This synovial change leads to joint and tendon damage by both chemical and mechanical forces. For the patient with mild or moderate involvement, the disease is most often controlled by careful maintenance of good general health, rest, controlled exercise, and the milder anti-inflammatory medications. Some patients' diseased joints are uncontrolled by such measures, and the condition progresses to serious multiple joint inflammatory reactions that may be uncontrolled even by intra-articular corticosteroids. Further, these changes go on to multiple and variable joint deformities.

Synovectomy, the removal of diseased synovium from a joint, was first done for tuberculosis before the turn of the century. It is the most common of the operative procedures for rheumatoid arthritis and is part of almost every reconstructive procedure. When done before erosion and cartilage thinning have occurred in the joint, it appears to extend the functional life of that joint for a considerable period. Around the wrist, the removal of tenosynovium may preserve tendon function.[23]

There are two questions to be answered in the treatment of the patient whose disease is resistant to usual and sound conservative means. Which patient should be selected for surgery? When should an operation be suggested? To the first, the patient should be one who can clearly understand the objectives and limitations of surgery, who realizes that it is not curative, and who wants it enough to be able to carry on the fairly rigorous postoperative rehabilitation program that will be required of him. As to the second question, when a specific joint is enlarged for three to six months and makes no response or worsens under good exercise and drug management, a synovectomy should be considered seriously. It is at this phase, before there is serious joint degeneration, that synovectomy offers the best relief and hope for the future of the joint. While the presence of articular erosive change, a later phase, does preclude the promise of relief and restoration of function by operation, this must be considered a salvage procedure to one degree or another.

1. Synovectomy

Synovectomy as a solitary procedure is most often done at the knee, possibly because swelling here is very apparent and knee pain is quite disabling. When done early, some excellent results have been obtained. When done after articular damage has occurred, temporary relief for a year or two may be satisfactory, but degenerative changes ensue and secondary procedures such as "total knee" may be required. Tenosynovectomy is often required at the dorsum of the wrist to prevent tendon damage. Painful elbows may often regain function through synovectomy, and the shoulder, more often involved than suspected, should receive consideration. Similarly, the ankle joint seldom gets the attention it deserves. Persistent swelling about an ankle joint associated with pain is the usual indication of synovitis of that joint. Weight-bearing x-rays both in the anterior posterior and lateral projections can be most useful in evaluating the extent of joint damage. If it is minor, synovectomy can do much to preserve function of the ankle.

Synovectomy has been especially useful in some of the related collagen diseases such as psoriatic arthritis. This condition is often accompanied by hydrarthrosis, which can be relieved by excision of the synovium. It is occasionally useful in the enlarged knee joints of juvenile rheumatoid arthritis.

2. Arthroplasty

In some patients, ligamentous and articular destruction continues and extensive multiple deformities may develop in spite of careful conservative management. Realizing fully that surgery is not in any way a curative process, various joint reconstructive procedures can decrease pain, increase strength, and maintain or restore function. Such patients are first placed on a carefully supervised exercise program, rest, and medication. One cannot wait until the disease process is quiescent, for this may never occur. Since there is multiple extremity involvement, it is necessary to formulate a careful plan of combined surgical reconstruction so that the patient can complete a program as quickly as possible with as little discomfort and as few anesthetic experiences as possible.

Painful, horn-like calluses under the metatarsal heads occur frequently in rheumatoid disease, caused by upward dislocation of the base of the proximal phalanx on its respective metatarsal head. The Hoffman operation, consisting of resection of a portion of the metatarsal head and of the proximal phalanx, effectively overcomes this problem. This condition is frequently associated with hand deformities. When this is the case, two surgical teams can correct one hand and two feet under one anesthesia in

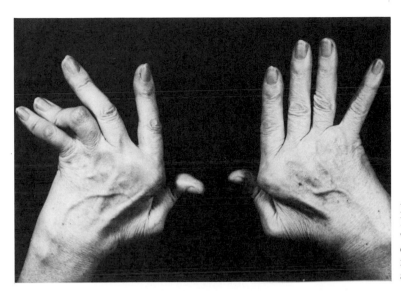

FIGURE 8a
Rheumatoid hands with
wrist synovitis, ulnar
drift deformities of
fingers, and the typical
attitude of the thumb.

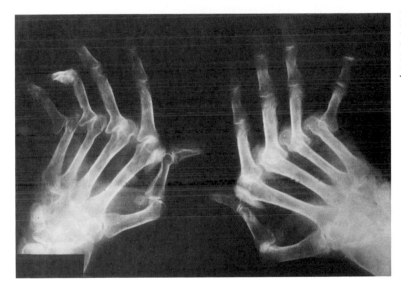

FIGURE 8b
X-ray views that reveal
dislocation of all
metacarpophalangeal
joints.

the properly selected patient. Other combinations of double extremity operations can be done according to the individual need. When deciding on such operations, it is important to judge not only the patient's temperament, but the type of rehabilitation for transfer activities, crutches, or toilet care that may be necessary in the postoperative period.

While relief of pain in the feet can provide the greatest satisfaction, the relief of pain, restoration of function, and improvement of appearance in hands and wrists are probably more important. Persistent synovitis in the metacarpophalangeal joints, with erosion, destruction, and muscle imbalance, leads to ulnar drift deformity of the fingers with dislocation of the phalanges beneath the metacarpal heads (Figures 8a, 8b). Reconstruction

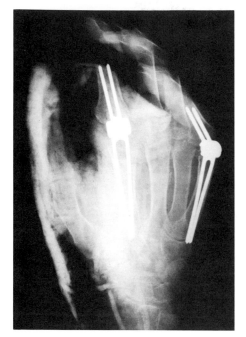 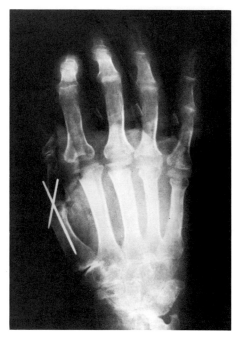

FIGURE 9a—Metallic hinge (Flatt) prosthesis at the second and fifth metacarpophalangeal joints.

FIGURE 9b—Silastic implants or "spacers" at the metacarpophalangeal joints. The crossed Kirschner wires immobilize the arthrodesis of the metacarpophalangeal joint of the thumb.

may be by resection arthroplasty, arthrodesis, or implant (Figures 9a, 9b). Similarly, where early synovectomy has not been done, there may be dislocation of the metacarpophalangeal joint of the thumb with resultant severe disability.[24]

Unchecked synovitis at the wrist can produce serious disability. Tenosynovitis in the extensor tendon at the dorsum of the wrist may lead to extensor tendon rupture, particularly of the ring finger, little finger, and thumb. This can be prevented by a dorsal tenosynovectomy at the wrist joint and resection of the distal ulna (Darrach procedure).[25] Persistent swelling and edema of the fingers may be indicative of deep synovitis within the small intracarpal joints. Synovectomy, done with ligamentous reinforcement before articular destruction occurs, will protect the wrist from further damage.

On the palmar side, synovitis of the flexor tendon sheaths in the fingers may cause limitation of flexion or locking in flexion or extension. Eventual tendon rupture is possible. At the volar aspect of the wrist, synovitis of the flexor tendon sheaths may produce median nerve compression (carpal tunnel syndrome), resulting in pain, thenar atrophy, and eventual tendon rupture. Prophylactic synovectomy in these areas depends upon early recognition of the anatomic changes and selection of the appropriate synovectomy. The

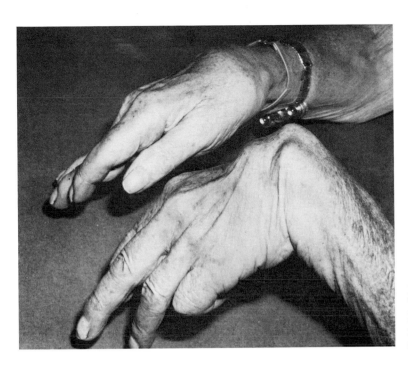

FIGURE 10
The rheumatoid wrist.
Dorsal synovitis on the
right. Total dislocation
on the left.

important signs of volar synovitis at the wrist are flattening of the thenar eminence and flattening of the base of the palm, with bulging proximal and distal to the transverse carpal ligament. Further, hypesthesia and pain in the median nerve sensory distribution (thumb, index, long, and one-half of the ring finger), often missed because of the pain of arthritis, are diagnostic. Delay of nerve conduction by electrical testing is confirmatory evidence of nerve compression. The ulnar nerve may occasionally be involved. Advanced destruction of carpal bones with dislocation of the wrist (Figure 10) requires arthrodesis for relief.[26]

Bulging synovitis at the elbow with crepitus on any motion and tenderness at the radial head are indications for synovectomy at the elbow joint.[27, 28] Increased range of motion can usually be obtained even though articular cartilage may be greatly thinned or destroyed. This procedure, combined with synovectomy at the wrist and Darrach procedure, may further increase the range of pronation and supination possible in a forearm. In juvenile rheumatoid arthritis total ankylosis of the elbow may occur. Fascial arthroplasty will restore motion to this essential joint.[29, 30]

At the shoulder, synovial bulging may occur in front of or behind the deltoid margin. Such enlargements may be substantial. Synovectomy can be accomplished by either anterior or posterior approach; if articular cartilage is present, the procedure will be very effective. If there has been advanced joint destruction and limitation, the Neer or similar prostheses are useful. In the ankylosed joint of juvenile rheumatoid arthritis, increased shoulder motion can be accomplished by resection of the outer end of the clavicle, a very simple procedure.

In the lower extremity, pain and swelling may occasionally be significant in the tarsal joints and in the ankle joints. If early synovectomy has not been done at the ankle, arthrodesis will probably be the treatment of choice. This is also true of the smaller joints in the foot.

The most troublesome of all joints of the lower extremity are the knees. Here, synovectomy seldom is done as early as it should be, largely because of the patient's reluctance. Failing this and with articular destruction established, articular replacement procedures are necessary, as described in the discussion of the osteoarthritic knee. They will vary according to individual needs, but generally the total knee procedures promise the most for the future of the rheumatoid condition. Severe varus or valgus deformities can be straightened by hinge prostheses. Rarely an osteotomy is required to correct very severe flexion deformities. Arthrodesis of the knee for a rheumatoid patient is to be avoided as it produces tremendous stress on other joints.

For serious rheumatoid involvement of the hip joint, total hip replacement has become the treatment of choice. Synovial enlargement is seldom recognized early enough for synovectomy to be beneficial. With articular thinning, degenerative changes will follow any operation that does not replace both sides of the joint. Fixing the two sides of the prosthesis to the pelvis and femur avoids many of the problems of absorption seen with the cup or femoral head prosthesis.

Finally, any complaint of pain in the neck or occiput of a patient with rheumatoid arthritis should be carefully heeded.[31] Synovitis of the facet articulation in the cervical spine can produce instability and nerve root compression. The first cervical vertebra may displace forward upon the axis so that the odontoid process moves posteriorly in the ring of the atlas and crowds the spinal cord posteriorly. Further down at the mid-cervical level, vertebral displacement and dislocation may occur as a result of synovitis. In these situations even a slight injury may have a fatal outcome. Cervical x-rays, especially lateral projections, are indicated whenever neck complaints are present and when there is severe generalized involvement by the rheumatoid process. For some patients with this type of involvement, carefully molded cervical "Minerva" neck collars may in time stabilize the spine, but where any change is suspected cervical spinal fusion should be undertaken.

D. Summary

In conclusion, one must recognize that many of the disabilities of osteo-arthritis can be avoided or minimized by early recognition and correction of static mechanical abnormalities. Further, it is realized that the majority of patients suffering from one of the rheumatoid diseases will not require surgery because of adequate physical and medical therapy or because of the limitations of the disease itself. However, for those with severe disability there are ever-increasing means of reducing pain and of restoring strength and function by surgical means in most parts of the body.

Although specific diseases were used as examples in the foregoing discussion, the principles presented apply generally to most forms of arthritis.

REFERENCES

1. *Rogers, W. A.: Fractures and dislocations of the cervical spine,* J. Bone Joint Surg. 39-A: 341, April 1957.

2. *Cloward, R. B.: The anterior approach for removal of ruptured cervical disks,* J. Neurosurg. 15:602, 1958.

3. *Heberden, W.:* Commentaries on the History and Cure of Diseases, 2nd edition, London, 1803.

4. *Stecher, R. M. and Hauser, H.: Heberden's nodes,* Amer. J. Roentgen. 59:326, 1948.

5. *Eaton, R. G., Dobrunski, A. I., and Littler, J. W.: Marginal osteophyte excision in treatment of mucous cysts,* J. Bone Joint Surg. 54-A:909, June 1972.

6. *Muller, G. M.: Arthrodesis of the trapezio-metacarpal joint for osteoarthritis,* J. Bone Joint Surg. 31-B:540, November 1949.

7. *Goldner, J. L. and Clippinger, F. W.: Excision of the greater multangular bone as an adjunct to mobilization of the thumb,* J. Bone Joint Surg. 41-A:609, June 1959.

8. *Darrach, W.: Forward dislocation at the inferior radio-ulnar joint, with fracture of the lower third of the shaft of the radius,* Ann. Surg. 56:801, 1912.

9. *Phalen, G. S.: The carpal-tunnel syndrome,* J. Bone Joint Surg. 48-A:211, March 1966.

10. *Levine, D. B., Wilson, P. D., Jr., Czerniecki, A., and Lim, W. N.: Diagnosis of Congenital Dislocation of the Hip in the Newborn. Film presented at the American Academy of Orthopaedic Surgeons Meeting in 1971.*

11. *Smith-Petersen, M. N.: Arthroplasty of the hip: a new method,* J. Bone Joint Surg. 21:269, April 1939.

12. *Charnley, J.: Total prosthetic replacement of the hip,* J. Med. Sci. 8:211, 1968.

13. *Bauer, G. C. H., Insall, J., and Koshino, T.: Tibial osteotomy in gonarthrosis (osteo-arthritis of the knee),* J. Bone Joint Surg. 51-A:1545, December 1969.

14. *Coventry, M. B.: Osteotomy of the upper portion of the tibia for degenerative arthritis of the knee,* J. Bone Joint Surg. 47-A:984, July 1965.

15. *MacIntosh, D. L. and Hunter, G. A.: The use of the hemiarthroplasty prosthesis for advanced osteoarthritis and rheumatoid arthritis of the knee,* J. Bone Joint Surg. 54B:244, May 1972.

16. *Gunston, F. H.: Polycentric knee arthroplasty,* J. Bone Joint Surg. 53B:272, May 1971.

17. *Walldius, B.: Arthroplasty of the knee using an endoprosthesis, Acta Orthop. Scand.* 24 (Suppl.):*43, 1957.*

18. *Young, H. H.: Use of a hinged vitallium prosthesis for arthroplasty of the knee, J. Bone Joint Surg.* 45-A:*1627, December 1963.*

19. *Mazas, F. B. and GUEPAR: Guepar total knee prosthesis, Clin. Orthop.* 94:*211, July-August 1973.*

20. *Jordan, H. H.:* Orthopedic Appliances, *New York, Oxford University Press, 1939, pp. 66–128.*

21. *Molded ankle braces. In* Orthopaedic Appliance Atlas, *Ann Arbor, J. W. Edwards, 1952.*

22. *Crenshaw, A. H., ed.:* Campbell's Operative Orthopaedics, *St. Louis, C. V. Mosby, 1971, pp. 1808–1825.*

23. *Straub, L. R. and Wilson, E. H., Jr.: Spontaneous rupture of extensor tendons in the hand associated with rheumatoid arthritis, J. Bone Joint Surg.* 38-A:*1208, December 1956.*

24. *Inglis, A. E., Hamlin, C., Sengelmann, R. P., and Straub, L. R.: Reconstruction of the metacarpophalangeal joint of the thumb in rheumatoid arthritis, J. Bone Joint Surg.* 54-A:*704, June 1972.*

25. *Straub, L. R. and Ranawat, C. S.: The wrist in rheumatoid arthritis, J. Bone Joint Surg.* 51-A:*1, January 1969.*

26. *Carroll, R. E. and Dick, H. M.: Arthrodesis of the wrist in rheumatoid arthritis, J. Bone Joint Surg.* 53-A:*1365, October 1971.*

27. *Inglis, A. E., Ranawat, C. S., and Straub, L. R.: Synovectomy and débridement of the elbow in rheumatoid arthritis, J. Bone Joint Surg.* 53-A:*652, June 1971.*

28. *Torgerson, W. R. and Leach, R. E.: Synovectomy of the elbow in rheumatoid arthritis, J. Bone Joint Surg.* 52-A:*371, March 1970.*

29. *Unander-Scharin, L. and Karlholm, S.: Experience of arthroplasty of the elbow, Acta Orthop. Scand.* 36:*54, 1965.*

30. *Dee, R.: Total replacement arthroplasty of the elbow for rheumatoid arthritis, J. Bone Joint Surg.* 54B:*88, February 1972.*

31. *Crellin, R. Q., Maccabe, J. J., and Hamilton, E. B. D.: Severe subluxation of the cervical spine in rheumatoid arthritis, J. Bone Joint Surg.* 52B:*244, May 1970.*

CHAPTER 9

Practical Aids for Evaluating Treatment Progress

Charley J. Smyth, M.D., M.A.C.P.
Professor of Medicine and Head
Division of Rheumatic Diseases
University of Colorado School of Medicine
Denver, Colorado

CHAPTER 9

Practical Aids for Evaluating Treatment Progress
Charley J. Smyth, M.D., M.A.C.P.

A. Introduction

Today's therapy for the rheumatic diseases is significantly more effective than that of even a decade ago. Ten years is a brief span in the history of man's suffering from the mysterious group of maladies we call rheumatism. But in this short time, remarkable progress in relieving pain and improving function in these potentially crippling diseases has been made.

The great forward strides in controlling gout exemplify these advances. Acute gouty attacks typically respond promptly to either phenylbutazone or indomethacin. Recurrent episodes can be prevented and tophi decreased by effective uricosuric agents, and tophi and kidney stones can be rapidly eliminated by blocking the synthesis of uric acid with allopurinol.

Equally noteworthy are the tremendous contributions of orthopedic reconstructive procedures. Pain and paresthesia in the arthritic hand are quickly relieved and function restored following carpal tunnel release. The reparative operations on the hips and knees using bone cement have contributed more true progress toward improving patient comfort and function than any other area of patient care.

These and other useful surgical procedures have greatly improved the functional ability of many arthritic patients who would have been considered hopeless cripples only a few years ago, and have led to a remarkable change in attitude among physicians from one of pessimism to one of optimism.

Because currently available therapy is only partially satisfactory, the search for more effective and safer agents for treating and preventing various types of arthritis continues at an increasing rate. As this research intensifies, new and better testing protocols are being developed. It is not the purpose of this chapter to describe the protocols in detail; however, the following discussion of tests and techniques used to evaluate new agents should be helpful to practicing physicians.

B. Tests of Inflammation and Function

1. Objective tests

In an effort to resolve some of the wide differences of opinion regarding the best way to reach a reliable evaluation of new agents, attention has been focused upon the development and use of objective measurements that yield quantitative data. However, most of the so-called objective tests do have some subjective influences. The following tests are commonly used for determining the degree of joint inflammation and functional ability.

a. Inflammatory index

This is an estimation of the overall inflammatory activity of the joints, based upon a clinical grading of swelling, heat, redness, tenderness, pain on motion, and fluid.

Paired joints are judged as a unit, and the amount of each element of inflammation is added to form a numerical expression. The sum of these measurements is expressed as an "inflammatory score" or index. Although not completely objective, this simple method permits an evaluation of the amount of synovitis present at any one time.

Previously published studies have shown that data obtained in using this test are reliable and sufficiently sensitive to express the activity of rheumatoid arthritis. There is a minimum of physician error. This test has been sufficiently used to evaluate the potency of several commonly used anti-inflammatory drugs, and the data obtained can be dealt with by statistical methods.[1,2,3]

b. "Activity Index" of Lansbury

This is widely used in drug trials to follow the course of patients with rheumatoid arthritis.[4] It is based on six fully reversible and quantifiable items, as follows:

- ▢ three subjective or interview items:
    duration of morning stiffness
    hours after rising when fatigue begins
    daily number of aspirin tablets needed for pain relief

- ▢ three semi-objective items:
    grip strength
    articular index
    Westergren sedimentation rate

Details of this test system with its latest modifications by Mainland and Sutcliffe can be found in Chapter 26 on Methods for Evaluating Rheumatoid Arthritis in the 1972 edition of *Arthritis and Allied Conditions* by Hollander and McCarty.[5]

c. Joint swelling

This is a consistent sign of synovitis, and the degree of enlargement of the fingers can be tested by using a steel jeweler's tape to determine the maximum size of the proximal interphalangeal joints. Another reliable test of the swelling of each hand (including the wrist) and each foot (including the ankle) depends upon the principle of water displacement using special hand-volume and foot-volume plastic tanks.[6] The accuracy of this apparatus is less than one percent of error for measurement of hand volume and 1.5 percent for foot size.

d. Joint temperature

In the search for an additional objective test of joint inflammation that would eliminate observer error, the internal temperature of human knee joints was investigated by Hollander and Horvath in 1953.[7] In three patients with rheumatoid arthritis they recorded decreases of 0.2 to 0.8° C in the internal temperature of these joints three hours after 0.6 g of oral aspirin. Other investigators using infrared scanning thermography have reported that the skin temperature rise associated with inflammatory joint disease is 3 to 5° C.[8,9,10] Thermography has also been shown to be of clinical value in the response of rheumatic patients to drugs and may well come to play a part in assessment before and after surgery.[8] Recently we have been using a skin contact probe developed at the University of Colorado by Guadagni, Kreith, Smyth, and Bartholomew.[11] It has a response time of 20 seconds and a reproducibility of ±0.01°. In six patients with rheumatoid arthritis, the results of skin temperature measurements correlated well with other clinical tests of joint inflammation (inflammatory index, ring size, and grip strength, Table 1).

Patient No.	n	Inflammatory Index	Grip Strength	Ring Size	Knee Circumference
1	9	0.894	−0.927	0.917	0.630
2	13	0.878	−0.852	0.757	0.436
3	13	0.873	−0.561	0.136	*
5	15	0.901	−0.748	0.809	0.436
6	17	0.892	−0.829	0.718	−0.083

*Not recorded

TABLE 1
Objective Clinical Tests of Joint Inflammation
Correlated with Skin Temperature
(Correlation Coefficients in 5 Rheumatoid Patients)

e. Articular tenderness

A simple instrument for precise quantification of articular tenderness is a spring-plunger gauge called a dolorimeter.[12] It has been shown to be useful when applied over small and large joints in the clinical evaluation of anti-inflammatory therapy. This method is partly subjective and depends upon the patient's willingness to cooperate.

f. Strength of grip

The power of the hand grip is a test of hand function. To measure it, we use a specially constructed mercury manometer that will register to 550 mm Hg, enabling us to record a wide range of variability encountered in normal and diseased subjects. A loosely rolled cuff of an ordinary sphygmomanometer with the balloon filled with air to 20 mm Hg will, upon squeezing, indicate hand strength by the height of the mercury column. This test of function is not entirely objective, and is affected by the patient's mental attitude, by the time of day, and by the amount of handwork having been done just prior to testing. More reliable grip strength data are obtained by taking the average of three tests done in rapid succession.

g. Walking time

The time it takes the patient to walk 50 feet (checked by a stopwatch) is a measure of joint function in the lower extremities. This distance has been found in this clinic to be a more useful test in measuring drug influence than the 25-foot walking test previously used. Patients are allowed to use a cane or crutches if necessary.

h. Technetium joint scanning
The radioactive isotope technetium or sodium pertechnetate is a gamma emitter with a short half-life and is safe for repeated administration. After intravenous injection, the counts over inflamed joints rise rapidly to a peak within 30 minutes. These counts have been used as a measure of joint inflammation and can be reduced by anti-inflammatory drugs.[13,14] By adding peak counts over a number of joints, a "technetium index" has been shown to correlate with a clinical index of disease activity.[15]

2. Subjective tests
a. Duration of morning stiffness
This determination is made by patient interview. The time at which the patient usually arises is noted. If stiffness is present, the time when this symptom wears off or when he "limbers up" is noted, and the duration estimated. This is one of the subjective items used in the rheumatoid activity index of Lansbury.[4]

b. Daily number of aspirin
A record is made of the average daily number of aspirin tablets taken for pain and not from habit. It is difficult to get the arthritic patient with chronic disease to keep an accurate daily record of the number of aspirins taken. If the collection of these data is supervised with great care and the patient is intelligent and cooperative, it has been shown to give reliable quantitative information.

c. Activities of daily living (ADL)
To gain a comprehensive assessment of the functional ability of an arthritic patient, a series of objective tests of activities of daily living has been found useful. A testing system described by Lowman[16] in a rehabilitation setting included 106 separate functions. A similar but less complex plan is one used by Robinson in a rheumatic disease unit. His activities of daily living system has proved to be helpful in determining ability to use public or private transportation, to walk, stand, and climb stairs.[17] These systems require considerable equipment, personnel, and time, and have little or no place in studies designed to determine the results of specific drug therapy or surgical procedures.

3. Evaluations of specific joints
a. Knees
Studies have been designed to assess the results of specific surgical procedures in arthritic patients. An example is the evaluation of the end results of

synovectomy of the knee in rheumatoid arthritis. Although there is general agreement that synovectomy should be performed early, most published studies do not allow one to draw conclusions regarding the true value of this procedure at any particular stage of the disease process.

A recent study by Geens and associates[18] used three measures to evaluate the results after a study involving 31 synovectomies in 23 patients. First was an analysis of the patient's own estimate (excellent, good, fair, poor). He used a 100-point scale similar to Larson's hip evaluation sheet.[19] A quantitative rating of 90 was excellent, 80 or more was good, and 70 or more was considered fair; a score under 50 was poor. Next, benefit was estimated by using a local inflammatory activity index based on ten criteria as derived from the 30-point score of the American Rheumatism Association Committee on Diagnostic and Therapeutic Criteria. A score from 0 to 30 was obtained, allowing a compatible quantitative rating of disease activity in the involved knee before synovectomy and at the time of follow-up. Finally, the examiner expressed his opinion, based on a list of eight criteria, including activity score and functional score, range of motion, pain, swelling, instability, flexion contracture, and progression of the disease seen roentgenographically. Arbitrary levels were determined for each of these eight criteria, and the results were classified as excellent, good, fair, or poor. This method for recording results following local therapy of knee joints in arthritic patients is highly recommended for anyone planning a quantitative investigation.

b. Hands

Many methods have been proposed for evaluating the disability of the arthritic hand. A rapid and simple method for expressing changes in a quantitative way is that of Treuhaft, Lewis, and McCarty,[20] which was designed to assess the structural and functional changes in the rheumatoid hand. Its use is also applicable to other arthritic conditions of the hands, and in evaluating the results of local medical and surgical therapy. Accurate estimates of range of hand motion with goniometry were considered unobtainable and extremely time consuming. Therefore, they were not included in this method of hand evaluation.

C. Role of Laboratory Tests

Only a few laboratory tests have any value in determining the influence of therapeutic programs for rheumatic diseases.

1. Sedimentation rate

This test is accepted by most observers as one of the most reliable criteria of disease activity in rheumatoid arthritis and its variants—especially ankylosing spondylitis, systemic lupus erythematosus, and rheumatic fever. In polymyalgia rheumatica, the sedimentation rate is unusually high; it falls to or toward normal as the disease activity subsides. This test can help in deciding when to discontinue or modify drug therapy. It is a reliable index of rheumatoid joint inflammation suppressed by long-term gold therapy, but has no statistical significance in short-term drug trials in gout, septic arthritis, Reiter's syndrome, tenosynovitis, and bursitis. It does not parallel the improvement in the objective test of joint inflammation following immunosuppressive therapy in patients with rheumatoid arthritis.

2. Synovianalysis
The number of white cells is a valuable guide in following the response to antibiotic therapy in septic joints. With satisfactory response, serial aspirations and total white cell counts will return to or toward normal as other signs of acute inflammation subside. Failure of the total leukocyte count to return to normal is an indication to either change the antibiotic or resort to surgical drainage.

3. Synovial fluid glycolytic enzymes
Bartholomew has shown that the enzymatic activity of three glycosidases (β-N acetylglucosaminidase, β-glucuronidase, and β-galactosidase) is markedly elevated in inflammatory joint effusions.[21] Estimates of these enzymes correlated well with the clinical status of the involved joint and the clinical response to intra-articular steroid therapy, thus offering a possible method for quantifying inflammatory joint disease.

4. Blood counts
Whenever certain drugs are used in arthritic patients, periodic total white cell counts are necessary to monitor the hematopoietic response. With gold, it is recommended that a complete blood count, including platelet estimations, be done before every second injection. Although infrequently administered today, roentgen therapy for ankylosing spondylitis requires total white cell counts before and once or twice weekly during therapy to avoid bone-marrow suppression.

With the increasing clinical use of immunosuppressive drugs (azathioprine, methotrexate, cyclophosphamide, and chlorambucil) in systemic lupus erythematosus, severe progressive rheumatoid arthritis, polyarteritis nodosa, polymyositis, and scleroderma, frequent and regular determinations of complete blood cell counts, including platelet estimations, are essential in the regulation of dosage and in following the degree of bone-marrow suppression. Following splenectomy in Felty's syndrome, the total leukocyte count usually increases rapidly, but may slowly return to the previously low level within six to nine months.

5. Muscle enzymes

In polymyositis, dermatomyositis, and the newly described "mixed connective tissue disease,"[22] there is a significant elevation of the serum levels of various enzymes that reflect skeletal muscle fiber damage.[23,24] Pearson has found that transaminases (glutamic or pyruvic—SGOT or SGPT), creatine phosphokinase (CPK), and aldolase are sensitive indicators of muscle damage, and that lactic dehydrogenase (LDH) is somewhat less reliable.[23] These enzymes often return promptly toward normal as the myopathic process responds to corticosteroid therapy. Their decline may precede clinical improvement by several weeks, and conversely the rise of these enzymes in the serum may foretell a relapse of the disease by as long as six weeks.

6. Uric acid determinations

The level of the serum urate followed at intervals of a few months to years is a well recognized way of judging the effectiveness of uricosuric therapy—probenecid or sulfinpyrazone—in chronic gout. Also, the serum urate level is used as a dependable guide in the management of chronic gout with allopurinol. If the level of the serum urate is kept at or slightly below normal, recurrent episodes of acute gout can be greatly reduced in number or even eliminated. In tophaceous gout, when the serum urate levels are maintained at or near normal, there is a consistent reduction in the size of the uric acid deposits. With adequate therapy, further progression of renal damage can be checked; recently we have obtained convincing evidence that existing reductions in renal function may be greatly improved.

The 24-hour urinary excretion of uric acid is normally less than 500 mg. The amount of uric acid excreted in the urine is increased to two or three times the normal value with uricosurics. This is another reliable test to help maintain a hyperuricemic patient in a more normal metabolic balance.

7. Anemia

In chronic arthritis, either primary or secondary to other diseases, anemia is a common finding. The type of anemia that occurs as a part of chronic connective tissue disorders is usually normocytic and normochromic. This anemia will improve with either a spontaneous remission or with satisfactory control of the active disease through therapy. When blood loss results from gastrointestinal irritation or ulceration, either spontaneously or from the use of salicylates, steroids, or other anti-inflammatory agents, the resulting anemia will by hypochromic.

D. Serial Radiologic Examinations

The use of repeated roentgenographic examinations has a limited place in most short-term therapy evaluation studies. However, in chronic gout with bony tophi, it may be of value to demonstrate the rate of urate absorption from bony tophi. A reduction in the size of bone erosions in rheumatoid arthritis following cyclophosphamide therapy has been claimed.[3] Radiologic examinations at six-month intervals are part of the multi-center knee and hand synovectomy study being supervised by a special committee of the American Rheumatism Association. In this study, an attempt is being made to determine if the operated joints are different from the control (unoperated) joints, as reflected in the changes in joint space narrowing, deformities, osteoporosis, and bony erosions.

E. Summary

Every practicing physician knows that few arthritic patients can be cured. There is, however, general agreement that with comprehensive and continuous care, only a limited number need become helpless invalids. The increasing search for better therapy has all but eliminated the suffering due to acute and chronic gout, and has greatly reduced the frequency of uric acid stones. Also, the marvelous advances in orthopedic surgery have culminated in the highly successful total hip replacement. These are clearly major advances in the treatment of arthritis.

The problem in evaluating new therapeutic programs is not in recognizing such dramatic benefits as these, but in accurately estimating the less striking benefits of some anti-inflammatory drugs and procedures in such diseases as rheumatoid arthritis. It is here that even a small degree of improvement is gratefully received by the patient. Progress is being made on a broad front to speed up the flow of effective, safe drugs from the laboratory to the patient.

As methods for evaluating therapeutic responses become more objective, it will be feasible to screen promising new treatments more rapidly and more efficiently. In the quest for ultimate cures in the large group of rheumatic diseases, the concerned physician should never forget that any relief, however small, will be welcome provided the risk is reasonable.

As noted in Chapter 1, the major objectives of treatment are to obtain sustained relief of pain and stiffness, to suppress joint or other connective tissue inflammation, to prevent deformities, but *mainly* to preserve function. If one method of therapy has failed to achieve adequate results, alternative means should be tried. This is the essence of "therapeutic resourcefulness."

REFERENCES

1. Smyth, C. J. and Clark, G. M.: Phenylbutazone in rheumatoid arthritis, J. Chron. Dis. 5:734, June 1957.

2. Smyth, C. J.: *A method of drug evaluation in rheumatoid arthritis: results with phenyl-butazone, oxyphenylbutazone, cortisone, and prednisone, Ann. N.Y. Acad. Sci.* 86:292, 1960.

3. Smyth, C. J., Bartholomew, B. A., Mills, D. M., and Steigerwald, J. C.: *Cyclophospha-mide therapy of rheumatoid arthritis, Ann. Intern. Med.* 78:833, May 1973.

4. Lansbury, J.: *Report of a three-year study on the systemic and articular indexes in rheu-matoid arthritis: theoretic and clinical considerations, Arthritis Rheum.* 1:505, 1958.

5. Hollander, J. L. and McCarty, D. J., Jr.: Arthritis and Allied Conditions, *8th edition,* Philadelphia, Lea & Febiger, 1972, Chapter 26.

6. Smyth, C. J., Velayos, E. E., and Hlad, C. J., Jr.: *A method for measuring swelling of hands and feet, Acta Rheum. Scand.* 9:293, 1963.

7. Hollander, J. L. and Horvath, S. M.: *Effect of vasodilating and vasoconstricting drugs on the temperature of normal and arthritic joints, Arch. Phys. Med.* 34:162, March 1953.

8. Gershon-Cohen, J., Haberman-Brueschke, J. D., and Brueschke, E. E.: *Medical ther-mography: a summary of current status, Radiograph. Clin. N. Amer.* 3:403, 1965.

9. Haberman, J. D., Ehrlich, G. E., and Levenson, C.: *Thermography in rheumatic diseases, Arch. Phys. Med.* 49:187, April 1968.

10. Viitanen, S.-M. and Laaksonen, A.-L.: *Thermography in juvenile rheumatoid arthritis, Acta Rheum. Scand.* 16:91, 1970.

11. Guadagni, D. N., Kreith, F., Smyth, C. J., and Bartholomew, B. A.: *Contact probe for skin temperature measurements, J. Phys. E.* 5:869, 1972.

12. McCarty, D. J., Jr., Gatter, R. A., and Phelps, P.: *A dolorimeter for quantification of ar-ticular tenderness, Arthritis Rheum.* 8:551, August 1965.

13. Dick, W. C. et al.: *Indices of inflammatory activity, Ann. Rheum. Dis.* 29:643, 1970.

14. Collins, K. E. et al.: *Radioisotope study of small joint inflammation in rheumatoid arth-ritis: radioactive technetium (^{99m}Tc) uptake in the proximal interphalangeal joints and the effects of oral corticosteroids, Ann. Rheum. Dis.* 30:401, 1971.

15. Oka, M., Rekonen, A., and Ruotsi, A.: *Tc-99m in the study of systemic inflammatory activity in rheumatoid arthritis, Acta Rheum. Scand.* 17:27, 1971.

16. Lowman, E.W.: *Rehabilitation of the rheumatoid cripple: a five year study, Arthritis Rheum.* 1:38, 1958.

17. Robinson, H. S. and Bashall, O. A.: *Functional assessment in rheumatoid arthritis, Canad. J. Occup. Ther.* 29:123, 1962.

18. Geens, S. et al.: *Synovectomy and débridement of the knee in rheumatoid arthritis, J. Bone Joint Surg.* 51-A:626, June 1969.

19. Larson, C. B.: *Rating scale for hip disabilities, Clin. Orthop.* 31:85, 1963.

20. Treuhaft, P. S., Lewis, M. R., and McCarty, D. J.: *A rapid method for evaluating the structure and function of the rheumatoid hand, Arthritis Rheum.* 14:75, January-February 1971.

21. Bartholomew, B. A.: *Synovial fluid glycosidase activity, Scand. J. Rheum.* 1:69, 1972.

22. Sharp, G. C. et al.: *Mixed connective tissue disease—an apparently distinct rheumatic dis-ease syndrome associated with a specific antibody to an extractable nuclear antigen (ENA), Amer. J. Med.* 52:148, February 1972.

23. Pearson, C. M.: *Polymyositis, Ann. Rev. Med.* 17:63, 1966.

24. Rose, A. L. and Walton, J. N.: *Polymyositis: a survey of 89 cases with particular reference to treatment and prognosis, Brain* 89:747, 1966.